CHRISTINE OLSEN was born and educated in New Zealand. She worked as a radio producer for Radio Television Hong Kong until 1985, when she came to Australia and began working in documentary film. Her production credits include the three-part television series *Riding the Tiger* and *Hephzibah*, which won two AFI awards including Best Documentary and the Silver Wolf Award for Best Documentary in Amsterdam. *Rabbit-Proof Fence*, which she wrote and produced, is her first feature script.

D1331660

.

rabbit-proof fence

the screenplay   christine olsen

Adapted from the book
Follow the Rabbit-Proof Fence
by Doris Pilkington Garimara

Currency Press, Sydney

First published 2002 by
Currency Press Ltd,
PO Box 2287, Strawberry Hills,
NSW 2012, Australia
enquiries@currency.com.au
www.currency.com.au

Reprinted 2004

In accordance with the requirement of the Australian Media, Entertainment and Arts Alliance, Currency Press has made every effort to identify, and gain the permission of, the artists who appear in the photographs which illustrate this screenplay.

NATIONAL LIBRARY OF AUSTRALIA CIP DATA
Olsen, Christine.
Rabbit-proof fence: the screenplay
ISBN 0 86819 655 X.
1. Aborigines, Australian – Fiction. 2. Moore River Region (W.A.) – Fiction. 3. Jigalong Region (W.A.) – Fiction. I. Title.
A822.3

Cover design by Kate Florance, cover image courtesy of Becker Entertainment.

All production stills that appear in the text are courtesy of Jabal films. (Photographers: Mervyn Bishop, Penny Tweedie, Matthew Nettheim, Lisa Tomasetti and Graham Shearer.)

Printed by Hyde Park Press, Richmond, SA

Contents

Christine Olsen.

Writer's Note

Christine Olsen

This is the first screenplay I have ever written. Somehow this seems important for this script. I knew I didn't know anything and I remember thinking, 'Well I'm just going to write it like I write for myself'.

Doris Pilkington Garimara had already recognised her mother's journey for what it was: a truly great story. Molly and her two cousin-sisters were 'removed' from their desert home in 1931 and taken down to a native settlement outside of Perth. The three girls, under the leadership of Molly, ran away and walked 1600 kilometres back to their home. As Molly said, 'We didn't like that place. I wanted Mother'. They found their way home by following the rabbit-proof fence, which runs north-to-south across the entire continent. Doris wrote the story, which was published as a book called *Follow the Rabbit Proof Fence* and I got the film rights to the book. So, as I say, the story was already there. Now all I had to do was write the script.

It was at this point that I got an inkling of what lay ahead of me. As I began to research the period, as my head began to fill up with thoughts and ideas, as the project began to take me over, I began to understand what my task really was: to find out why this particular story so moved me. Why was Molly's story also my story? As I continued researching, writing, my mind never quite clear of it, I found myself saying, 'Aaah, so this is what the story is about'. And then, six months further along the track, I would think, 'No, this is what it is about.' And each discovery became a layer in the story.

At first it seemed that this was a classic fairytale: three children stolen away by a wicked witch and taken to her house. In this house everyone has been put under a spell of forgetfulness. The longer the children are there the more strongly the spell works on them. The three sisters escape and are pursued by the vengeful, angry witch every inch of the way. They must use all their cunning to evade her and get back home.

And then I thought, 'No, this is a war story. The country has been invaded and taken over. Now, even deep in the hinterland, the invaders are reaching out and taking away the children. They are placed in camps from which only three escape. To get back home they must cross through enemy-occupied territory never knowing who their friends are, who is out to get them.' And this territory I knew very well. It was where I had been brought up.

I grew up in a small country town and as a child, I would go with my family to visit my father's sister who lived on a farm. One Sunday when we were there an old tramp came to the door and my aunt piled a plate with food and took it out to him. He sat at the back door eating. It seemed to me that my father's sisters and brothers, my father himself, would not have thought any differently than the people then. 'Racism' was not a word they would have known. And so the script became peopled by my family.

Eventually I came to realise that my story/Molly's story was about home. I was working on the script in Sydney. I had my ideas about the story but I knew they were not enough. Doris had taken me to Jigalong several times to meet Molly and Daisy, the two girls who'd made it back home. They were now 85 and 79. Jigalong is a remote desert community, difficult to get to, cut off from the world during the 'wet'. Doris and I would make the long journey from Perth, stay a few days and then leave. But I knew I had to spend a long time just being there. Then Doris told me she was going to Jigalong for a funeral. I said, 'Can I come too?'. We went and stayed with Molly for three weeks. And that was what nailed it for me. Three weeks of doing nothing but give myself over to the rhythms of the place. Three weeks of taking Molly her tea and just sitting. Three weeks of walking at dawn in the desert with Dora and Joan and Amy. On the way back Doris and I stayed at the caravan park at Newman. I went for my early-morning walk into the hills. Somehow, now, the land was terribly alive for me. I didn't get lost but I heard some strange sounds and I was terrified. I hid behind an incline and waited, my heart pounding. 'This is how those girls would have felt', I told myself, 'all the way back'.

How lucky I was throughout this whole experience. Is 'luck' the right word? I had Doris who took me to Jigalong and looked after me.

I had my dear friend, John von Sturmer, a great expert in these matters, gently guiding me. 'I will just say one thing,' he would say and it would be a thing of great wisdom and insight.

It's all very well never to have written a film script before, but you do need some taking in hand. Thanks to Claire Dobbin, my project officer at the Australian Film Commission, who, among other things, made sure that I got myself the right script editor. That was Alison Tilson. There, you see? Luck and good management. Thanks Alison.

Above all I had the people of Jigalong. To me, going there, it felt as if people made room for me. Get in the back of the truck crowded with girls and babies and grannies, people made room. Sit on the ground to talk, people made room. I wasn't fussed over. I wasn't anything special. I was simply included. For that I feel greatly privileged.

Christine Olsen
January 2002

Everlyn Sampi as Molly.

A Jigalong Diary

Christine Olsen

About three hundred people live at Jigalong. There is a store, a school and a clinic. To get there you drive into the desert from Newman. You must ford several rivers and if it rains the road can be blocked for weeks.

This is an extract from a diary I kept when Doris and I went with her son Ricky for a family funeral. It was very hot – the rainy season. That visit we stayed for around three weeks.

SATURDAY

We arrive at Newman and the little truck comes to pick us up. We load onto the tray at the back and bounce out here. My legs go to sleep because the camera bag is on them. The truck is packed – all female except for Ricky. Little girls, bigger girls, girls sharing one cigarette, two grannies. Everyone close and touching. Laughing, whispering, close. People sitting between people's legs, arms around waists. Easy.

We stop at the creek crossing. 'No swimming' shouts one of the grannies, Dora – she can see rain up ahead. Wants to get home. We catch fish – tiddlers – and three big girls swim – how could they resist? How do I resist?

Back in the truck. Nearly there. A puncture. All unload. Two girls catch a tiny lizard thing. 'There', says Doris, 'that's that …' It's the little lizard that kids would tie up outside a bough shelter and pretend was their dog! It rains a bit and some of the girls get under a piece of material. Shapes under it, pulling the material over them.

We arrive at Molly's house – what luxury – a shower, toilet, clean room for Doris and me. We've displaced a family – mother, father and two kids, one a tiny little new-born baby. They sleep in the main room and don't seem too fussed. The baby wakes once towards the morning.

Today, Sunday. Sitting on Molly's bed. Sitting. Not too hot yet – nice breeze. Sandra has just turned up for the funeral and she and Molly are wailing. The dogs bark in sympathy.

MONDAY

A long, hot, quiet day. The men's business is taking place. It takes precedence over the funeral. We are sitting, waiting. Then we are sitting waiting for the store to open. The video – Jackie Chan – is blaring forth. A strong, upright, painted man turns up. His beard and hair are all covered with red clay and his upper chest is painted black – a shovel shape covering most of his sternum and upper chest.

Then we hear that the store is open so Ricky and I wander over and sit there and wait along with everyone else. Eventually we give up and come back to Molly's.

'Should've waited till we seen the plastic bags,' says Ricky. The store opens and we go over. It's crowded with people. There are no shopping baskets so everyone stacks all their goods on a shelf and then moves them closer to the till.

At night we sit outside and watch the lightning. I can hear, very faintly, the men singing near the creek.

Videos, Toyotas, heat, people sitting.

Today is the funeral. Doris warns me that there might be fighting and I should move away very quickly from the funeral area. Everyone sits bent over on the ground, wailing. Then half of them leave for the church. It's probably cooler inside. Molly and Daisy stay lying in the sun. We move to the shade and wait. Hours later they come from the cemetery. There's no fighting, just a bit of wailing and we all go home.

Later in the afternoon. It's very hot. Molly is sleeping in her bed on the verandah having sprayed herself with No Frills Fly Spray. Cocky Boy is trying to eat himself out of his cage. Two men, one with a guitar, lounge on chairs under a tree across the way. The sun beats down. Puffy clouds. Funny to think that the sky is the one changeless thing.

The girls stroll past – one or two of them have taken my eye. Raeleen is very cheeky, very sexy. Yesterday she was wearing a coordinated outfit – very sporty. Black shorts and singlet with a yellow stripe running wide up the side. She has short black hair. She smokes. The other one – I don't know her name – has short, curly brown hair. Not as confident as R but lovely, smiley face. Neither of them very open. Today someone else is wearing Raeleen's yellow-and-black shorts.

It's Molly's 'daughter' who has died. Actually it's a niece.

Doris says that when she came looking for her mother they said, 'That one down there – the fair one.' (Doris was 'taken' from her mother when she was four and reunited with her twenty years later.)

Sounds – dogs barking, kids laughing, the language – sometimes like bubbling water, sometimes screamed by the young women, birds. When the generator is off, a lovely stillness.

I don't think anyone is going to care much about the film – they prefer Jackie Chan, Wesley Snipes and Arnie.

Information seems to be a different thing here. Who organised the funeral, when is the shop open, when and where do the buses run, why is one of Molly's dogs tied up and none of the others? I learn not to ask but to wait to be told what I need to know.

WEDNESDAY

I walk over to see Daisy. She and Molly used to swing off a rope into the river. 'Naked.' She laughs. Then they would put their 'drawers' on. I imagine that I can still see the little girl in her.

Raeleen's yellow-and-black shirt has just walked past – on the girl with the curly hair.

Daisy showed me the sand game – shapes made in the sand using the edge of your hand and your fingers. The man – straight line – the wife – curved line – several wives and children – and dogs – and the camp 'Maia'. She's laughing about the curves, the women, the girls looking for the man.

Molly has been bad tempered over the last couple of days – no tobacco – but the truck has just come in. I find myself going to the shop several times a day for something to do. I am surprisingly happy here doing almost nothing.

THURSDAY

Yesterday Dora came over with some other women, said they were going walking early this morning. I invited myself along. Got up at first light and walked over to meet them. Picked up a stick against the dogs. Looked for 'the yellow house' and found it! Everyone still asleep on beds outside. Went and waited past Dora's house because I thought they'd collect me as they came by. Waited, waited, then walked by again. Still asleep. Walked back and the next-door neighbour woman shouted out to me. Dora woke up and we three walked out to the airstrip. On the way Joan said, 'Look at the fishes' – hundreds of little dead silver fishes were lying scattered on the ground. She says they come down when it rains! Everyone says, 'Fish in the creek. Children catch fish'.

Joan talking about the story: 'How did they know how to get home?'

Me – 'Rabbit-proof fence'.

Joan – 'If it wasn't for that they couldn't have got home. Good thing, that fence'.

Idea that the rabbit-proof fence led them home. I said, 'And you know what the trouble was with the rabbit-proof fence? People left the gates open'. We laugh. Story of the fence intersecting with their lives. Fathers – worked on the fence. Good thing. No rabbit-proof fence, no Molly or Daisy. No way to get home. Something so clear and obvious.

We sit around outside, talking. Doris is a great storyteller. She is describing an old man trying to eat a frankfurter but the bread roll was too small for the hot dog so that, every time he bit, it squirted out the other end and fell on the ground. He'd pick it up, dust it off, put it back. Finally someone called out, 'What? That thing alive?'. Everyone laughs.

Simplicity/magic. Fishes falling out of the sky.

Maria – 'You like it here?'

Me – 'Yes. It's very peaceful. You like it?'

She – 'Yes'.

Videos, tele-shopping, Hollywood.

Evening – a walk down to the creek with Ricky. I say the clichéd thing about how long has this creek been running along here? Clichéd thoughts, composing the opening scene – the stillness, the reflection, dappled water, ancient rocks, primordial *but* realise to people here this is ordinary. It's not beautiful. 'Beautiful' is what visitors say. Dogs barking, kids playing, adults screeching. This is ordinary, it's home. They don't see it with an outsider's eyes. Thinking this morning as I walk along with Joan, seeing her black feet – I am as old as she is – we are all part of this world recycled over and over again. Joan's observation that it was the rabbit-proof fence that meant they could find their way home. Nothing mystical about that. Three little girls following a fence.

I've lent Molly my roll of mosquito cream. She was in the kitchen looking at the can of Mortein, shaking it. Luckily it was empty.

THURSDAY

Morning walk. Joseph shouts out to me, wants to know where I'm going. 'To Molly's' I tell him.

'Cadigan?' he says.

'No, Molly's house next to Cadigan's.' I make the sign with my hand.

'She your mother?' he asks and then proceeds to try and work out my *relationship* to Molly. Finally I give in and say, 'Yes, she's my aunty'.

Then he says – by now he's walking with me and I notice *again* what a beautiful child he is – that I better not take my stick with me because of the dogs.

'No', I say proudly, 'they're Molly's dogs, they know me.' And sure enough they come out wagging their tails at me. He stands watching. I *had* better be careful, though.

SUNDAY

Molly talks more in the morning. This morning she said that workers on the rabbit-proof fence gave them food and directions. They walked only at night along the fence. During the day they walked in the scrub away from it. Also, once they were nearly caught and they hid in the hills.

Very hot afternoon but it doesn't rain. I take some meat to Joan's and walk with her and her husband out to the airport. He has the most amazing face.

I think about how important *people* are here – what's going on – relationships. On one level nothing happens – we sit and wait, every day unravels – lovely coolish morning, hot, hot day and the evening. But on another level things happen all the time – dogs, people, the store, the electricity. Joan's mother's broken leg.

It's raining now – lovely. (What did Dora say about her granddaughter? 'She talks like a whitefella' – 'It's lovely, Nan.')

TUESDAY

Waiting for the ride into town. Is the road open? I walk over to Dora's under a little Barbie umbrella that I found at Molly's. Leeandra and five other little girls, muddy, wet, meet me coming the other way, all crowded under their umbrella. Then they run off, the last little one puckering her lips up for a kiss.

WEDNESDAY

Think this is it. Early morning walk with Dora and Amy. There are lots of seeds in piles on the road from last night's storm. Dora's going to come back and collect them. At 4.30, when I woke, the sky was just beginning to lighten – and then a misty, moisty morning. Now the sun's really out and it's hot. Packing up again – lucky it's so easy. A little frog had his bum poking over the end of the bed. He turned to look at me, gulping quite fast. Called in to see Joan on my way back from the walk – sat outside with her and measured her head for the hat I'm going to send her.

Ricky's out of the shower. I'd better go and clean my teeth.

MAIN CAST

Molly   EVERLYN SAMPI
Daisy   TIANNA SANSBURY
Gracie   LAURA MONAGHAN
Moodoo   DAVID GULPILIL
Molly's Mother   NINGALI LAWFORD
Molly's Grandmother   MYARN LAWFORD
Mavis   DEBORAH MAILMAN
Constable Riggs   JASON CLARKE
Mr Neville   KENNETH BRANAGH

Directed by Phillip Noyce
Screenplay by Christine Olsen
Produced by Phillip Noyce & Christine Olsen

How the script relates to the finished film

The published screenplay is the final shooting script, however further changes usually occur due to the conditions of production and contributions made by cast and crew. The following excerpts from *Dead Heart* by Nick Parsons show how differences in the finished film are noted.

1. The scene numbers on the left are the original numbers in the shooting script. Numbers in braces on the right indicate the actual position of the scene in the film. ⌐

SCENE 120 EXT. THE AIRSTRIP – WALA WALA. DAY.{121} ◄

2. The * symbol indicates that in the film the scene as written formed only part of the scene in the finished film. Thus scripted scenes 61 and 62 each form part of film scene 63. ⌐

SCENE 61 INT. THE KITCHEN – THE DOCTOR'S RESIDENCE. NIGHT.   {63 *} ◄

The penny drops. Sarah shakes her head in mock disbelief.

{SARAH: Some anthropologist.}
CHARLIE: She was having an affair?
SARAH: Of course she was having an affair.

SCENE 62 INT. THE OFFICE – THE POLICE STATION. NIGHT.
                                                    {63*} ◄

The video screen shows Kate with the body. By now Sarah has opened her medical bag and is saying something to Kate.

3. If a scene from the shooting script was cut from the film it has no final film version scene number. ⌐

{SCENE 105 INT./ EXT. TOM'S FOUR-WHEEL-DRIVE – THE SPINIFEX PLAIN. DAY.

The engine roars as Ray urges his vehicle on.}

4. Braces around text, whether dialogue or a scene description, indicate it is not included in the finished film.

{*A luncheon meeting of the Perth Women's Service Guild. A darkened room, the soft hum of a lantern slide projector. Shapes of women.*

Perth, Australia, 1931.}

On one wall a black-and-white photograph is projected onto a screen. Some Aboriginal women beggars stand beside a train. They look desperately into the camera. They are dressed in ill-fitting, rough clothes. Two of the women have half-caste children slung on their backs.

The cultured English voice of Mr Neville, aged 51, rises above murmurs of discomfort from the audience.

NEVILLE: {The sad end of what was once a truly magnificent race, the Australian Aboriginal, now a derelict, dispossessed people. Yes, it is shocking, but there is nothing we can do about it.

   A pause as the disturbing image is taken in.}

Notice the half-caste children. {These children are our special responsibility.} And there are ever increasing numbers of them. What is to happen to them? Do we allow the creation of an unwanted third race? Should the coloureds be encouraged to go back to the black?

   A click and a flash of light as the slide is replaced. An Aboriginal woman with her little girl. The image comes into focus. They look out at the women.

Or should they be advanced to white status to be absorbed into the white population? {Here you see a first cross half blood mother with her quadroon child.}

   Neville stands beside the projector, looking at the image, arms at his side.

Time and again I have been asked by some white man, 'If I marry this coloured person, will our children be black?' As Chief Protector I have the responsibility of approving or objecting to such marriages and here is the answer.

   He changes the slide. The screen flashes a brilliant white and then another photograph – a family of three generations – smiles out.

Three generations – half-blood grandmother, quadroon daughter and octaroon grandson. As you can see, in the third generation, or the third cross, no sign of native origin is apparent. The continued infiltration of white blood finally stamps out the black colour, {which, unfortunately, when all is said and done, is what people really object to. And in my lengthy experience of hundreds of families I do not remember observing any throwback to the black.}

Murmurs from the women.

The Aboriginal is simply bred out.

A flash. White, manicured hands adjust the focus, spotless cuffs. Neville's face is lit from below as he looks up at the picture.

A photograph of Moore River Native Settlement, the church on the hill.

He steps forward with a pointer. Now half his face has the photo imprinted on it. He taps the picture.

Now we come to Moore River Native Settlement. Ladies, most of you will be familiar with the work that we are doing here – the training of domestic servants and farm labourers – and I want to thank you for your continuing support. Hundreds of half-caste children have been gathered up and brought here to be given all the benefits that our culture has to offer.

He steps out of the light, looks at his audience. He speaks with great conviction.

For if we are going to fit and train these children for the future, they cannot be left as they are. {We want to give them a chance. We want to teach them right from wrong, so that they will be no different from you and I.} The native must be helped in spite of himself.

SCENE 2 EXT. THE DESERT. DAY.   {4}

(Note: in the finished film Scene 1 consists of a card that reads 'Western Australia 1931. For 100 years the Aboriginal Peoples have resisted the invasion of their lands by white settlers. Now, a special law, the Aborigines Act, controls their lives in every detail. Mr A. O. Neville, the Chief Protector of Aborigines, is the legal guardian of every Aborigine in the State of Western Australia. He has the power to remove any half-caste child from their family, from anywhere in the state.' Scene 2 is an aerial shot of the desert, which comes to focus on the Jigalong homestead, with a voice over from Molly, speaking in dialect: 'This is a true story – story of my sister Daisy and my cousin Gracie and me when we were little. Our people, the Jigalong mob, we were desert people then, walking all over our land. My mum told me about how the white people came to our country. They made a storehouse here at Jigalong – brought clothes and other things – flour, tobacco, tea. Gave them to us on ration day. We came there, made a camp nearby. They were building a long fence.' In Scene 3 young Molly looks around the trees at the billabong. She continues the voice over: 'My Dad was a white man working on that fence. The white people called me a half-caste.')

Birds and wind. Scrubby desert plants. Red soil. Molly, fourteen, is walking with her mother Maude, 32. A little hunting party is spread out behind them. Molly's, Gracie's and Daisy's grandmother Frinda, 65, and Gracie's mother Lilly, 28, look for goanna tracks. Gracie, ten, and Daisy, eight, trail behind. A couple of kangaroo dogs race ahead. Molly puts her hand lightly on Maude's arm. Maude turns to look at her. She smiles at Molly. Behind them Frinda spots some tracks. She calls to the others. All dialogue is in language.

FRINDA: Over here.

> *Maude and Molly begin to walk towards Frinda but the tracks disappear. (Note: in the finished film, the goanna is found in a tree fork and the dialogue in the remainder of this scene has been paraphrased.)*

[*To Maude, shouting*] Keep looking. Maybe in that direction.

LILLY: [*calling*] It went somewhere.

> *Frinda walks, head down, carrying her digging stick. She picks up the trail again.*

FRINDA: Over here.

> *She pokes with her stick.*

He went there, in that hole.

> *Maude and Molly arrive. Maude has a look.*

MAUDE: It's here alright.

> *Lilly comes up.*

LILLY: This is the place.

> {*The dogs return and stand, expectant. Gracie and Daisy arrive, watch. Frinda kneels, ready to dig. Gracie moves in closer. Frinda looks sharply at her, speaks in language.*}

FRINDA: Don't stand there.

> {*Gracie steps back and Frinda begins to dig, sending the stick hard into the ground. The earth is soft and falls away easily into the goanna's burrow. Everyone is watching, quiet. Only the sounds of a bird far off and the dogs, eager-eyed, panting. Molly plucks a leaf from the tree, rolls it in her fingers, makes a pretend cigarette. Puffs on it. She crushes the leaf, holding it up to her nose. She stands looking out over her country, smelling the leaf.*}

> *Molly's point of view: the land stretches out to the horizon, trees, grasses. Not far off, small, distinctive hills. A large hawk, black and brown, flies into view. Everything slows down, slow-motion. It hovers in the air. Comes to land on a tree.*

> *Now everything returns to normal motion. {From this point on all the dialogue will be in English unless specified.} Behind her Frinda calls out.*

Hey Molly, that hawk, that spirit bird.

(Note: in the finished film this action is included in Scene 3, and Frinda adds 'He will always look after you.') Molly watches as the bird flies off.

Maude takes over from Frinda, taps with her stick, begins to dig. The earth crumbles, opening even further. Molly, to one side, sees the back of the goanna as it lies curled around a tree root. She pounces, grabbing it by the tail, shouts.

MOLLY: He's here. He's here.

The kids peer into the hole, see the goanna's curved back. Molly holds the tail, straining on it. Maude looks up from her digging.

MAUDE: Hold it tighter in case it gets away.

The goanna clings to the tree root. Molly pulls as Maude loosens the earth around it. Finally it is pried loose and Molly can pull it free. She stands there, one slender arm high in the air, triumphant, laughing at the others. The goanna hangs at full stretch: long tail, fat, quivering underbelly, tiny splayed legs and snakelike head; a beautiful, golden-brown creature. Maude stretches out one of the tiny legs to reveal the body, smiles at Molly.

{Fat one.

Daisy and Gracie dance with excitement. Frinda nods her grudging approval. Maude takes the goanna and, holding it by the tail, whacks it on the head with her stick.}

SCENE 3 EXT. JIGALONG – OVERLOOKING THE CAMP. DAY.

{5*}

Constable Riggs, uniformed, and Arthur Hungerford, Superintendent of the Jigalong Depot, sit on their horses surveying the scene. They are hidden among the trees. As they watch, Molly and the little band of hunters walk back into the camp. Molly is carrying the dead goanna, Gracie and Daisy dance around her. Hungerford turns slightly towards Riggs.

HUNGERFORD: That's them … {Those three … The ones with the goanna.}

Both men continue to watch. (Note: in the finished film Hungerford adds 'Molly's the big one. The little one's her sister Daisy. The middle one's their cousin, Gracie.')

SCENE 4 EXT. JIGALONG – THE CAMP. DAY.   {6*}

Molly is carrying the dead goanna. Its tail drags along the ground. Gracie and Daisy dance along beside her. Ahead of them, their camp. Some bower shelters. Smoke from campfires. Dogs. Little children playing. Two Aboriginal men, Joshua and Thomas, are sitting by a fire. A little way off the large river gums which border the creek bed. One of the men calls out.

JOSHUA: Bring it here.

SCENE 5 EXT. JIGALONG – OVERLOOKING THE CAMP. DAY.

{5*}

Riggs and Hungerford watch from their horses.

RIGGS: Where are their fathers?

HUNGERFORD: Moved on. {Last I heard Craig was working the fence down south.

RIGGS: Well, anyway, Mr Neville's their legal guardian. It'll be up to him what happens to them.}

SCENE 6 EXT. JIGALONG – THE CAMP. DAY.   {6*}

The little procession is joined by two children. They throng excitedly around Molly as she walks over to Joshua. {He takes the goanna, holds the head so that it looks at Daisy.

JOSHUA: He's looking at you.

Daisy giggles, squirms away. Everyone laughs.}

At a distance, Hungerford and Riggs sit watching. Hungerford gives his horse a kick, edges it forward. Riggs follows.

(Note: in the finished film Frinda sees Riggs and Hungerford watching them. She instructs Molly to hide the kids and Riggs and Hungerford walk away. Lilly explains 'Policemen ... looking for half-castes.')

{Joshua looks up. His eyes show his disquiet. Everyone follows his gaze. Riggs and Hungerford bring the horses to a halt. Sit there, high on their backs. Molly moves over to stand close to Maude. The people wait. Quiet. Apprehensive. Hungerford looks over the faces. Finds Maude. Then Frinda and Lilly. Molly edges closer to Maude.

HUNGERFORD: Hello Maude, Frinda.

> *He nods at them. Gracie and Daisy edge behind Lilly. Hungerford turns to Riggs.* This is Constable Riggs.}

SCENE 7 EXT. THE VERANDAH OF NEVILLE'S OFFICE – PERTH. DAY.   {9*}

{*The back of a government office building. Around them other government buildings. In the distance a cityscape.*}

A number of Aborigines queue, chatting, at the foot of some steps leading up to a verandah. They are all dressed in their best, the men with brilliantined hair.

(Note: in the finished film this action is included in Scene 8 as Miss Thomas' point of view through the window.)

SCENE 8 INT. NEVILLE'S OFFICE. DAY.   {9*}

(Note: in the finished film Scene 7 is black-and-white footage of cars driving along a main street in Perth, Western Australia. Scene 8 shows cars and trucks at an intersection.)

A crowded, tiny room. Dozens of small wooden card drawers line the dark brown walls. A desk is crammed into one corner, record cards in neat piles on top of it. At the front of the desk an emu egg mounted on a silver dish. A clock ticks. Everything is ordered, quiet.

Neville, tie, waistcoat, his white shirt impeccably ironed, a narrow crease running down each arm. Above the starched collar a pink and white complexion, almost babyish, as if he has only just shaved. He sits at his desk writing on some cards. Beside them Riggs' letter and map and a folder.

A knock on the door and Miss Thomas, 37, comes in. She is carrying a pile of manila folders.

MISS THOMAS: The next batch. Nothing out of the ordinary.

> *She walks over to his desk. Begins to lay each folder on top of it, summarising them as she does so. Neville continues his writing.*

Two applications for Section Sixty-three exemptions … the police reports are there.

> *She taps the folder. He glances over at it. Selects a stamp and inks it.*

William Harris is applying for permission to marry …

Kenneth Branagh as Mr Neville.

She checks the form inside the next folder.

She's a half-caste also.

Neville stamps Riggs' letter. She lays the folder on the desk.

Mary Wilson is applying for permission to visit her child at Moore River ...

She puts the two last folders down. Glances towards the window.

She's quite agitated.

Neville writes a date on the stamp. Miss Thomas taps the top folder lightly.

Gladys Phillips has written for permission to buy some new shoes.

Neville flicks casually through the papers in the file.

NEVILLE: She had a new pair a year ago.

He gathers together Riggs' letter, the map and the folder. Holds them out to her. She takes them.

This report from Constable Riggs, on the three half caste girls at the Jigalong Fence Depot ...

He gathers the cards he's been writing on. There are three of them. He looks at them.

Molly, Gracie and Daisy. The youngest is of particular concern. She's promised to a full-blood.

He taps them together. Hands them to her.

I'm authorising their removal. They're to be sent to Moore River as soon as possible.

She turns, is walking out.

Oh, Miss Thomas.

She stops, turns to look at him.

Can you check that the rate for the police transportation is still eightpence a mile?

SCENE 9 EXT. THE RABBIT-PROOF FENCE – JIGALONG DEPOT. DAY.   {11}

The rabbit-proof fence. It stands straight, sturdy, its creosoted bottom-half buried in the sand, the grass well cleared to either side of it. It runs to the side of, and beyond, the Depot buildings which are some way off.

Molly, Gracie, and Daisy are playing near a young white fence worker, Reg, 24, who is replacing a piece of wire netting. Daisy and Gracie play against the fence, pulling themselves close to it, pushing off from it, while they interrogate him. Molly stands nearby, watching, waiting. Every now and then Reg glances over to her.

Some cockatoos squawk, fly over.

{*Daisy is educating Reg.*

DAISY: They devils, you know.

She looks at him very seriously and then, pointing over to some country, way over, tells him more.

That man's place. You can't go there. They catch you.

Reg appreciates the information.} *(Note: in the finished film Gracie tells Reg, 'That country over there, that's woman country. You can't go there. You get big trouble'.)*

REG: Mmm, I know.

Gracie and Daisy are still swinging on the fence. Molly twists a piece of grass in her fingers.

MOLLY: Which way your country? {Where you come from?}

Reg looks over to her. Nods south, along the fence.

REG: My country that way ... south. Long way.

Daisy leans back from the fence, her fingers entwined in the wire.

DAISY: Our dad's gone that way. He workin' too, on that rabbit fence.

Reg continues with his work.

GRACIE: How far this fence go?

REG: Right to the sea. Both ends, all the way, from here to the sea.

(Note: in the finished film he goes on: '... that way, right to the top of Australia. Longest fence in the world. And all the way to the sea down that way. Fifteen hundred miles long. Keeps the rabbits on that side of the fence, keeps the farmland on this side of the fence.) {*He stretches both arms out but they've lost interest. A bell clangs out. Molly flings the piece of grass away.*}

SCENE 10 INT./EXT. JIGALONG DEPOT – THE STORE ROOM. DAY.   {10}

Hungerford stands outside on the verandah. He is preparing for the weekly ration day hand out to the Aboriginals. A small pile of blankets, sacks of flour, sugar, tins of tobacco, tins of bully beef. {*He jots down numbers on a piece of paper, counting the blankets, tapping the tins with his pencil, murmuring under his breath.*} *(Note: in the finished film he rings a bell.)*

Constable Riggs, wearing his uniform – blue jacket, silver buttons, moleskin trousers, boots, leans against the door post, careful to stay out of sight, chewing a straw and watching.

{*Riggs' point of view: Molly, Gracie and Daisy are standing talking to Reg on the other side of the fence. As Riggs watches they begin to walk towards the depot.*

Hungerford looks across to the three girls, looks over at Riggs watching them.

HUNGERFORD: Where's the car?

Riggs takes the straw out of his mouth to answer, eyes still on the girls.

RIGGS: Round the back.

His eyes flicker to indicate the direction. Then he slides inside the door, out of sight.}

{SCENE 11 EXT. JIGALONG DEPOT. DAY.

A call. The three girls look over. Maude and Lilly, Gracie's mother, are strolling along the track towards the depot. Two dogs bound around the women, chasing each other, sniffing out game, racing through the scrub. Behind them two other Aborigines are coming from the camp. Gracie and Daisy call back to their mothers, begin to run to meet them. Molly saunters over, leans against Maude. Maude smiles at her.

MAUDE: I told you before. Keep away from that fence boy.

The woman and girls come through the gate in the fence, close it after them. They walk towards the Depot, the women relaxed, laughing.}

SCENE 12 EXT. JIGALONG DEPOT – THE STORE ROOM. DAY.

{12}

Maude and Lilly are chatting to Hungerford at the store room door, a sack of flour and a sack of rations at their feet. Four Aboriginal people wait a little distance away. Riggs is nowhere in sight. Hungerford nods towards Molly.

HUNGERFORD: She's getting to be a big girl.

LILLY: She be married soon.

HUNGERFORD: Mister Neville's been writing to me about her.

Maude darts a fierce look at him, clutches the bag of flour to her.

MAUDE: You tell that Mr Devil Molly stop here. She marry soon.

{*She lifts the flour onto her head and stalks off, turns to shout.*}

That Mr Devil he want half caste baby, he can make his own. [You tell him.]

The little party meanders its way back through the morning light towards the gate in the fence, Maude and Lilly giggling at Maude's boldness, hips swaying. [The dogs tear ahead of them.]

Molly walks behind them and Gracie and Daisy dance along in the rear, playing a game with a disc [of bark], throwing it to one another.

SCENE 13 EXT. JIGALONG DEPOT. DAY.

[13, 14, 15, 16, 17, 18, 19]

(Note: in the finished film Scenes 14, 16 and 18 are car interiors.)

It is Molly who hears the car first. She turns and stands watching as it bumps over the flat ground towards them, a blinding light flashing from the windscreen. She screws up her eyes against the glare. In the distance Gracie and Daisy look up from where they are scrambling in the sand to get the [bark] disc. Maude and Lilly turn, [the flour bag balanced on Maude's head.] They all stand and watch, curious, as the car makes its way towards them, weaving past shrubs, flattening the spinifex.

The sun reflects off the windscreen, masking the driver. It is still some way off when there is a loud 'thunk' as the side running board collects a buried stump. The car pulls to a stop. They watch as the door opens and Riggs steps out.

Maude and Lilly see the policeman, know instantly why he's come. They cry out low and urgently to the children, hurrying awkwardly towards the gate, clutching their bags to them. Gracie and Daisy are still playing with the disc. They look up at the women. Molly signs to them to come, then she too runs after the women.

Riggs is examining the running board.

Gracie and Daisy begin to run.

Riggs looks up. Sees the women making for the gate. He gets back in the car, revs the engine, speeds after them. Gracie and Daisy are running after the women and the little group is spread out, exposed, the car easily overtaking them. Riggs circles around, pulls up a little in front of them. The women are caught between the depot and the gate, trapped by the fence. They look frantically towards the camp, calling out shrilly. Molly steps close to Maude. The door opens. Riggs, one hand on the wheel, the other clutching some papers, levers himself out. He leaves the engine running, stands there, a white man in a policeman's uniform.

Ningali Lawford as Maude, Everlyn Sampi as Molly, Jason Clarke as Riggs and
Tianna Sansbury as Daisy.

RIGGS: Maude, I've come for the girls. {Orders from Mr Neville. They're to go to school.}

Lilly swings round, calling out desperately to Daisy and Gracie. They run and huddle behind her, peering out from around her skirt. Riggs opens the back door of the car. It swings open, cavernous. He strides over to Lilly and plucks Daisy from her skirts. Lilly swings the sack of goods at him but he fends her off, carries Daisy over to the car, puts her in the back. She sits on the edge of the seat, clutching onto the seat in front, legs dangling. Big eyes watching. {The dogs appear, snarling. Riggs lashes out at them with his boot. They back off, continue to snarl. Maude and Lilly call frantically to the camp. The car motor runs.

Now Frinda is running from the camp carrying a stick.} Riggs looks towards the camp, takes two steps, tears Gracie from Lilly, bundles her roughly in beside Daisy. Slams the door shut. They sit there, terrified, looking out the window. {Maude has hold of Molly, flour spilling over both of them. Riggs stands between the car and the women, waving the papers.}

I have the papers Maude. It's the law.

Frinda arrives with the stick. Riggs looks at her. Dismisses her.

There's nothing you can do, old lady.

Maude clutches Molly to her, eyes wide, disbelieving. (Note: in the finished film Maude continually cries out not to take her children.)

{MAUDE: That's my kid, my roan. I been grow her up. Nobody else.

Riggs takes a step towards them.

RIGGS: Mr Neville is their legal guardian.

Maude puts herself between him and Molly. She screams out at him, her face streaked with flour, a grotesque mask of fear.

MAUDE: Those girls our roan kids. Come from here.

She touches her stomach. Hungerford walks over. Stands there. Reg has stopped working. He is watching from a distance. Frinda looks at the policeman, raises the stick. Riggs reaches over, wrests the stick from her. She stands there, tiny, defiant but resigned.}

Molly is clinging to Maude. She watches as Riggs comes over. He towers over them, stick and papers in one hand.

RIGGS: It's the law, Maude. You got no say.

His arm reaches out, takes Molly high on the arm, drags her around to the other side of the car. She stumbles beside him, her feet leaving deep tracts in the earth.

She can see Gracie and Daisy huddling inside the car. Riggs pulls the door open.
Shoves her roughly into the back. The door slams shut.

SCENE 14 INT./EXT. RIGGS' CAR – JIGALONG DEPOT. DAY.
{20, 21, 22, 23}

(Note: Scenes 21 and 23 are Jigalong Depot exteriors.)

Molly looks out at Maude who is peering in the window, reaching out her hands to Molly,
shouting to her. {Molly tears at the door and the window. She can see Riggs's backside
through the windscreen as he bustles around to the driver's door.} Now the door opens and
Riggs gets in, his big face red and sweating. {He tosses the stick in beside him, adjusts
himself in the seat, pulls the door shut. He looks back at Molly. She is frantically scrab-
bling against the door. Riggs reaches his arm across and bangs the lock down, grunting with
the effort.} He revs the engine and the car begins to move, turning in a wide arc.

Molly watches as the desert turns. She hears the muffled sound of the women's wailing as
Maude and Lilly begin to run after the car. Gracie and Daisy sit in stunned silence beside
her. Maude and Lilly's faces appear, pressed to the windows, Maude's streaked with flour,
as they run alongside the car, tearing at the doors. Molly looks back and sees Frinda throw
herself to the ground. She sees the women drop off, one by one, as the car picks up speed.
They fall to the ground and lie there, face down, stretched out in grief. Frinda picks up a
stone and smashes it into her head.

{Riggs reaches for Frinda's stick. He tosses it out the window. The stick bounces once or
twice, then disappears from sight.} (Note: in the finished film this scene finishes with Neville's
voice over: 'As you know, every Aborigine born in this state comes under my control' and
then cuts to Scene 1 of the shooting script.)

SCENE 15 EXT. MOORE RIVER NATIVE SETTLEMENT. DAY.
{46, 47, 48, 49, 50}

A thousand miles south. Cold, bleak. The buildings of the Settlement uncared for. No
grass around them, only dirt.

Neville and the Superintendent of Moore River, Earnest Neal, 54, are inspecting the
outside wall at the back of the girls' dormitory. Neal is dapper, moustached. He carries a
riding crop which he taps against his leg. His little white dog scratches in the dirt beside
them.

Moodoo, a tall, black Northerner, powerfully built, dressed in policeman's jacket and old brown trousers, stands a little way off. Further off a few girls, one of them Tracy, hang around the dormitory.

Neal points out a broken board with his riding crop. (Note: in the finished film, this scene takes place after Olive is returned to the settlement, and the following conversation is referring to Olive's escape. When Neville refers to Moodoo's daughter, the film cuts between Moodoo and Tracey having her hair brushed by Miss Jessop.)

NEAL: They broke out of here. Usual story. Off to see their boyfriends at New Norcia.

He looks at Neville, watching for his reaction. Neville doesn't react. He's examining the broken board.

{Mission boys.}

He indicates Moodoo with the crop.

The tracker brought 'em back.

Neville steps back, carefully wipes his hands with a spotlessly clean, white handkerchief.

NEVILLE: Aah yes, Moodoo.

He looks over to him. Begins to fold the handkerchief.

Mr Neal informs me that your parole period is up.

Moodoo steps forward, nods.

And that you want to return to the Kimberleys. Is that right?

Neville is folding the handkerchief. He looks at Moodoo. Moodoo nods again. Neville glances over to Tracy in the distance.

Of course, your daughter is here, isn't she?

Moodoo looks at the ground. Neville weighs the folded handkerchief in his hand.

There would be no question of her going. She would have to stay here and continue with her training.

He considers. Moodoo waits. Neal fiddles with the broken board. Neville puts the neatly folded handkerchief in his jacket pocket.

I think for the time being it would be best for all concerned if you remained here Moodoo. I would be prepared to consider your case in a year or so ... but until then...

{*He begins to walk away. Neal goes with him, tapping the riding crop against his leg, a slight limp as he walks. Moodoo stands there. Neville takes a little notebook from his pocket. As they walk he refers to it.*

There's three little half castes on their way from the fence depot at Jigalong.
You'll need to keep a close eye on them. You know how it is, it takes a few
days for them to get accustomed to the place.

Neal swishes the crop.

NEAL: Yes, yes.}

The little white dog trots along behind Neal.

{SCENE 16 EXT. MARBLE BAR COUNTRY. DAY.

*Exquisite countryside. Deep blue sky, red hills, a towering hill, silence. A small plume of
smoke. Riggs' car is pulled over. A billy sits just off the fire. Riggs sits on a log, hat to the
back of his head, eating a piece of damper.*

*Molly, Gracie and Daisy are sitting huddled together. Daisy fiddles with some damper.
Molly gestures to her, tugs on her skirt, signs.*

MOLLY: [*signing, insistent*] Give me. Give it here.

> *Daisy very reluctantly, eyes on Riggs, hands the food over. Molly digs a hole in the
> sand behind her, keeping a watchful eye on Riggs, and buries the food in it. Gracie
> hands a tin of tea to Daisy. She slurps some down, hands the tin to Molly.*

> *Riggs finishes his tea, tosses the dregs on the fire, stands.*

RIGGS: If you gotta go, you girls better go now. I'm not stopping again.}

{SCENE 17 EXT. MARBLE BAR COUNTRY. DAY.

*Molly and Gracie squat behind some bushes. Daisy joins them. Their piss runs across the
sand. Daisy moves her toes out of the way, watches as it runs away from her. Molly looks
up from where she is squatting.*

*Molly's point of view: the distinctive little conical hills near Jigalong. She looks at
them for a long time. Riggs shouts. They can see his head through the bushes, standing by
the car.*

RIGGS: No tricks, you girls.

> *They stand, walk back, along the tire tracks in the red earth. Daisy walks close to
> Molly, whispers to her.*

DAISY: You took my bread.

MOLLY: Might be poison.}

{SCENE 18 EXT. NULLAGINE POLICE STATION. EVENING.

A light on in the policeman's house. The tiny barred window of the watch house.}

{SCENE 19 INT. NULLAGINE POLICE STATION – A CELL. EVENING.

Gracie and Daisy huddled together in a corner under a blanket. No mattress. Molly is standing, wrapped in a blanket, peering out through the narrow slit in the door.

Molly's point of view: blackness. A few stars.

GRACIE: Where we goin'?

> *Molly presses her face hard against the opening. Doesn't answer.*

DAISY: What gunna happen?

> *Molly turns away from the door, tears streaming down her face.*

MOLLY: We gunna die. Finish.

> *She throws herself down on the floor beside them, face down, hands tearing at her hair.}*

SCENE 20 EXT. JIGALONG. FIRST LIGHT.   {27}

Maude sits alone by a small fire, facing east, away from the camp. She is wailing, her cries carrying out towards the rising sun.

SCENE 21 INT. THE GUARD'S VAN. DUSK.   {25}

Molly sways on the wooden floor in the corner of the guard's van, watching through the barred window of the side door opposite as the land speeds past. The train clatters along. Gracie and Daisy are crammed in beside her.

{A policeman sits on a wooden seat across from them. Behind him, through the open door, a carriage with passengers. Molly's point of view: dissolve from countryside to sea as they travel through it. Dissolve to darkness.}

(Note: in the finished film Scene 26 is an exterior of the train steaming past. Scene 28 is the train passing through a gorge; Scene 29 is the children sleeping in a cage, Scene 30 is the train crossing a bridge at sunrise; Scene 31 is Gracie staring at the passing countryside while Molly and Daisy sleep.)

SCENE 22 EXT. MOORE RIVER – A ROAD. LATE AFTERNOON.

{32}

A small truck drives across the desolate country around Moore River.

{SCENE 23 INT./EXT. THE TRUCK. LATE AFTERNOON.

Molly sits on the floor in the back of the open truck, watching as the countryside passes on either side of her. Gracie and Daisy are slumped asleep beside her. They are all clutching new calico bags.}

SCENE 24 EXT. MOORE RIVER NATIVE SETTLEMENT. DUSK.{33}

(Note: in the finished film a supered title reads 'Moore River Native Settlement. 1200 Miles South from Jigalong'.) Molly watches out the side of the truck as they turn into the Settlement. In the evening light she can see a few run down buildings. The truck runs across some gravel and comes to a stop. The horn is sounded. Gracie and Daisy start awake. The truck door slams. Footsteps on the gravel. A lantern passes by the side of the truck. A woman's head, wearing a white nurse's headdress, peers in.

Gracie and Daisy cling on to Molly, terrified. Daisy whispers to her.

DAISY: A ghost.

> *It is Mrs Neal, the wife of the Superintendent and Matron of Moore River. Grey haired, 58, motherly. She is holding a lantern above her head.*

MATRON: You poor dears, such a long way. You must be exhausted. Come along. I'll take you straight to the dormitory.

> *(Note: in the finished film, with Matron's encouragement, the children cautiously hop down.)*

SCENE 25 EXT. MOORE RIVER NATIVE SETTLEMENT – THE DORMITORY. LAST LIGHT.

{34}

{Molly's bare feet squelch through the mud, stumbling in the dark, following the light. Gracie and Daisy cling onto her skirt.} Wooden steps up onto a verandah. They stand at a wooden door, bolted and padlocked. Matron fiddles with some keys, pulls the bolt.

SCENE 26 INT. THE DORMITORY. NIGHT.   {35}

A large room. Beds everywhere and faces squinting into the light. The lantern swings around, finds three empty beds with bare, dirty mattresses, a blanket folded on each.

MATRON: There's some beds.

> *The sounds of mice scampering. Matron swings the lantern to flush them out. The light passes over a bucket in the corner. {Molly puts her bag on the bed, Gracie and Daisy still clinging to her. The light goes out. The door shuts.*
>
> *Blackness.*
>
> *Sounds of the bolt sliding, the padlock clicking shut. Daisy whimpers. The whispers come from all around the room. 'Where you from?' 'What's youse names?' Molly does not answer. All three shiver in the same bed under a blanket.}*

SCENE 27 EXT. MOORE RIVER NATIVE SETTLEMENT. MORNING.   {36}

An overcast, miserable day. The whole settlement lies before us.

SCENE 28 INT. THE DORMITORY. MORNING.   {37}

Clatter, clatter, clatter. Molly starts awake. Lies, wide-eyed, in the bed. Gracie and Daisy are huddled into her.

SCENE 29 EXT. MOORE RIVER NATIVE SETTLEMENT – THE DORMITORY. MORNING.   {38}

Clatter, clatter, clatter. A black warden, George, 45, is running a stick along the length of the wall. He wears an old blue policeman's jacket, torn trousers, bare feet.

SCENE 30 INT. THE DORMITORY. MORNING.   {39}

{Sounds of the padlock being unlocked.} Molly looks around the room from her bed.

A roomful of beds filled with strange children, some with shaved heads, ringworm sores painted purple. Some are stirring, some are getting up, scratching themselves, their heads.

Kate Roberts as Matron.

Big girls are combing little girls' hair. There is shouting, laughing, calling out. Everyone wears the same coarse dress they have slept in. The bucket is in the corner. The windows are covered with mesh.

A bell rings. Loud.

A big girl, Nina, fifteen, her head shaven, comes across to the bed, stands there, looking down at them. She's carrying a stick.

NINA: Hey. Where you from?

> *All eyes turn to look at them. Molly shrinks down. Nina gives a short nod of the head.*

You'll get used to it.

> *She walks away, shouts at another girl, Tracy. She's half joking, half threatening.*

Hey, Tracker girl. Take that bucket outside. It's your turn, you lazy bitch. They'll belt you.

> *She takes a swipe at Tracy who looks defiantly at her then collects the bucket and carries it at arm's length out of the room. The bell rings again. Loud. Impersonal. Nina throws the stick on her bed, makes for the door. (Note: in the finished film Nina continues to boss the other girls around, finally asking Molly, Gracie and Daisy whether they are coming for breakfast.)*

SCENE 31 INT. THE DINING HALL. MORNING. {40}

{*Molly stands in a queue, Gracie and Daisy squeezed behind her.*} *A crowd of about forty children, boys and girls, ranging in age from four to fourteen, all dressed the same.* {*Miss Jessop doles out porridge onto tin plates. George patrols the room, stick in hand.*

Molly takes a plate of grey sludge and goes to sit on a bench. Gracie and Daisy squeeze next to her, Daisy's feet dangling down. There are no spoons, tins for cups. Everyone sits, waits. Silence.} *Miss Jessop stands,* {*ladle in hand,*} *closes her eyes, leads the grace. (Note: in the finished film, Miss Jessop prompts the children to bow their heads and close their eyes. When the film has finished she tells the children that 'there will be no talking'.)*

Molly's point of view: everyone closes their eyes, intones:

ALL: Thank you for the food we eat, thank you for the world so sweet, thank you for the birds that sing, thank you, God, for everything.

> *Molly watches as all the children stuff the porridge into their mouths and gulp down tea. She takes a handful, eats it. The only sounds are the clanking of tin plates and the sloshing of tea.*

Daisy picks out a lump of porridge, tries it, gags. She pushes the plate away, murmurs to Molly in language:

DAISY: Rubbish food.

Whack! The stick slams onto the table beside her. She jumps. George is standing behind her.

GEORGE: None o' that wangka here. You talk English. Now, eat.

The stick pushes the plate back to Daisy. She shudders. Whack! Comes the stick again.

Eat or I'll hold ya nose and force it down ya.

{*Daisy, tears welling, picks out a tiny piece of porridge, puts it in her mouth, shudders, retches. Molly pushes a tin of tea to her. Daisy, blinded by tears, gulps, swallows. Gracie, big-eyed, watches it all. George moves on. Molly deftly swaps plates with Daisy, begins to eat.***}**

SCENE 32 EXT. MOORE RIVER NATIVE SETTLEMENT – THE LATRINES. MORNING.   {41}

A section marked off next to the dunnies by some old sacking staked to form a square. Within it, Molly is being scrubbed vigorously by Miss Jessop. Gracie and Daisy stand shivering beside her. We can see from their backs, waist up. Beneath the sacking we can see their feet and a bucket. (Note: in the finished film Miss Jessop tells Molly: 'Keep still. I've got to scrub you. Let me see … Doesn't that feel better?'. When Molly doesn't respond, Miss Jessop prompts 'Yes, Miss Jessop' which Molly repeats, then 'Thank you, Miss Jessop' which Molly also repeats. Miss Jessop tells her 'That is much better', as the children's feet are seen standing in mud as Miss Jessop scoops another cup of water.)

SCENE 33 INT. THE SEWING ROOM. MORNING.   {42}

A small, unlined room. Wooden floor, wooden walls, shelves with piles of folded shifts, some canvas shoes. Five treadle sewing machines in a row. Phyllis, Irene and Gladys are sewing at the machines, their work in piles around them. Some younger girls of about ten to twelve sit on a bench, hand sewing. The machines whir, start and stop. May, fifteen, is tying the finished shirts into bundles with string and stacking them for collection. **{***Nina slouches against the door.***}** *Molly and Gracie stand, old blankets wrapped around them. Miss Jessop is kneeling, pulling an old shift over Daisy's head. Gracie whispers in language to Molly:*

GRACIE: New clothes.

Miss Jessop glances over to them.

MISS JESSOP: You speak English here. This is your new home.

She {stands,} throws two shifts {and three pairs of shoes from the shelves down} to Molly and Gracie.

Put these on.

(Note: in the finished film the scene begins with the line above as Miss Jessop approaches with three uniforms.) {She walks back along the row of machines, stopping at each to check their work. She glances out the window.

Miss Jessop's point of view: Matron is coming towards the sewing room. Miss Jessop makes a general announcement.

Remember, girls, it's Saturday today. Pay day.

Matron comes in. She's carrying a box of chocolates. She looks at Molly, Gracie and Daisy.

MATRON: They look just like Moore River girls now, don't they, Miss Jessop?

She looks over to Nina.

Nina, take them to the nursery. Show them how to sweep.

She begins to walk along the row of machines putting a few chocolates on each machine. The machines whir. The girls barely look up from their sewing.}

SCENE 34 INT. THE NURSERY. MORNING.   {44*}

A room filled with small empty enamel cots crammed together. Through the back door can be seen little children in a pen. Molly and Gracie sweep clumsily. (Note: in the finished film Nina stands by the door with a broom, telling Molly: 'Over here. Sweep it over here, to the door'.) {Daisy stands looking at two little babies in cots in one corner. Nina leans against the wall looking out a window. She gives a low whistle. Molly looks up, leaves the broom and goes to look out the window. Gracie and Daisy come to watch too.}

SCENE 35 INT./EXT. THE NURSERY. DAY.   {44*}

(Note: in the finished film this scene is from Nina's point of view.) {Molly's point of view:} a miserable figure of a girl of about fifteen, Olive, is trudging along the path. Behind her, slouched on his horse, is the powerfully built figure of the black tracker, David Moodoo. He sits easy in the saddle, careless, whip coiled before him. Other children watch from the

shadows of the buildings. As Olive and Moodoo draw near, Molly can hear Olive's snivelling. Moodoo takes his whip and prods her in the back. (Note: in the finished film Nina calls to Tracy 'Hey, tracker girl, your dad's bringing Olive back. He catched her'.)

SCENE 36 INT. THE NURSERY. DAY   {45*}

(Note: in the finished film this scene is on the verandah.) Molly turns to Nina.

MOLLY: She run way home?

> *Nina still watches as Olive and Moodoo go towards the boob. She turns to look at Molly, gives a derisive laugh.*

NINA: Nah, she jest run away to see her boyfriend.

SCENE 37 INT./EXT. THE NURSERY. DAY   {45*}

They all watch as the dapper, dandified figure of the superintendent, Mr Neal, comes around the corner. He is carrying a riding crop, which he taps against his leg. {His little white dog follows close on his heels. One of the babies begins to cry.} (Note: in the finished film Nina and Molly walk out onto the verandah. Neal asks Olive, as she cries, 'Did you really think you'd get away with it? Now stop that crying. You see what Miss Doyle has here? Olive, look at me. You see this here? The scissors? You should have thought about his beforehand'.)

{Olive stands waiting, head downcast. Moodoo sits on his horse. The baby continues to cry. Daisy looks anxiously around at it. The dog stands growling at the girl, hair bristling, as} Neal turns Olive and steers her round the corner with his riding crop. (Note: in the finished film Neal forces Olive into a shed, and Olive is heard crying out.) {The little dog leaps excitedly after them.

A bell rings out. Children begin to stream towards the dining room.}

SCENE 38 INT./EXT. MOORE RIVER NATIVE SETTLEMENT – THE BOOB. AFTERNOON.   {53*}

(Note: in the finished film Scene 51 is Molly, Nina, Daisy and Gracie sitting in long grass under trees. Molly asks Nina about the mothers of the babies in the nursery. Nina replies 'They got no mothers. Nobody here got any mothers'. Molly replies 'I got mother'. They leave to line up for church. Scene 52 is Molly and Daisy running to the boob, where Olive is heard crying.) Molly is standing pressed against the wall, peering through a gouged out

peep hole in the side of the boob. Daisy stands beside her, back to the boob, looking out.

A pair of black eyes, puffy with crying, looking up at Molly. Freshly shaved head. Olive crouched down on the dirt floor, arms around her legs, hemmed in by the tin walls of the tiny boob.

{OLIVE: What you looking at?

> *Molly is silent. Daisy tugs on Molly's skirt.*

DAISY: I wanna see. I wanna see.

> *Molly lifts her up, eye to the peep hole, little hands against the tin wall.*

OLIVE: What's your name?

> *Daisy can barely whisper her name.*

DAISY: Daisy.

> *A black hand grabs Molly by the back of the neck, hard, painfully, and pulls her away. Daisy drops to the ground. Molly is shaken, roughly, and then thrown. She stumbles, gets her balance and turns to look into the face of the black tracker, David Moodoo. He takes a step towards her, stands there, eyeing her.*

MOODOO: That'll be you next if you don't watch it.

> *Molly stands her ground. The tracker puts his face close to Molly's.*

I seen you already. You try anything, I'll get you.

> *Molly turns, flees, Daisy at her side.*}

SCENE 39 EXT. MOORE RIVER NATIVE SETTLEMENT. AFTERNOON.   {43}

A crowd of unkempt children, pudding-basin hair cuts, boys with no shirts, girls all dressed in the same shifts. Bare feet in the dirt. No grass. In the background the church hall.

Molly, with Daisy and Gracie, peers through the heads of a group of children. Daisy is on tip-toe trying to see. A little raggedy choir is singing 'Swannee River' to a small audience of adults: Neal and dog, Matron and Mr Neville, who stands awkwardly to one side, hat in hand. Miss Jessop conducts, mouthing the words.

CHOIR: 'Way down upon the Swannee River, far, far from home ...'

> *Molly whispers to Nina beside her.*

MOLLY: What they doing?

> *Nina whispers back.*

NINA: They singing for Mr Debil.

MOLLY: Which one Mr Debil?

{NINA: That one with the hat. Cup-and-saucer face.}

> *(Note: in the finished film Nina replies 'The one on the end on that chair'.) Molly takes a good look at him.*

> *The song finishes and Neville pats one of the children on the head, speaks to Miss Jessop. He takes out a pen and notebook from his pocket, steps over to confer with Neal. Neal clears his throat. Rocks back and forth on his heels.*

NEAL: The following children will come forward.

> *He cocks his head towards Neville as the Chief Protector reads a name to him.*

Tommy Grant.

> *A little boy is pushed forward. The crowd watches. (Note: in the finished film Neville says to Tommy 'This way, Tommy. Here' as Miss Jessop shepherds Tommy forward, prompting him to 'Stand up straight'. {Matron moves over to Tommy Grant, takes him by the arm and leads him over to Neville.} Neville lifts Tommy's shirt to look at the skin on his back.*

MOLLY: What they doing?

> *Nina speaks into Molly's ear.*

NINA: They lookin' for the fairer ones.

> *Molly turns to look at her.*

It's for Sister Kate's – they take the fair ones to Sister Kate's – they're more clever. They kin go to proper school.

NEAL: Molly Craig.

> *Molly looks at Nina. The girls all turn to look at her. Nina gives her a nudge.*

NINA: That you. Go on.

> *Molly stands there. Neal cranes to look into the crowd.*

NEAL: Molly Craig.

> *Nina pushes her forward. (Note: in the finished film Nina tells Molly 'Go on, get up …Hurry up, they'll whip you … they'll put you in the boob. Hurry up'. When Molly stands, Daisy clings to her and the Matron specifies 'Just Molly, please'. Nina pulls Daisy down, and tells her to sit down, as Matron encourages Molly towards Neal and Neville.) Molly steps forward, head down. Matron comes towards her, takes her by the arm, leads her over to Neville. Neville stands waiting, pen and notebook in one hand.*

NEVILLE: Come on. I'm not going to hurt you.

> *He takes a step to meet her, looks into her face.*

Molly, isn't it? I know it is all very strange, but after a few days you will feel quite at home here.

Molly looks down.

We're here to help and encourage you in this new world. Duty, service, responsibility. Those are our watchwords.

He reaches out a hand, moves the neck of her shift so that he can see the skin on her neck. She stands there, rigid, refusing to look at him. Neville turns to Matron, shakes his head.

No.

He begins to write in his notebook. Molly turns, head still down, but from the corner of her eye she is watching him, taking note.

{SCENE 40   INT. THE DORMITORY. NIGHT.

Molly lies awake, Gracie and Daisy curled beside her. Daisy is asleep. A little girl, Evie, six, is crying.

EVIE: Mummy. I want my mummy.

Molly looks round for her. One girl stirs, moaning. Nina calls out.

NINA: That you, Evie?

Molly can see Evie now, curled up on her bed.

Come here. And bring your blanket.

Molly watches as the shape of the little girl, still crying, slides out of bed and crosses the room.

Get in here … but no wetting.}

{SCENE 41   EXT. MOORE RIVER NATIVE SETTLEMENT – THE BOOB. NIGHT.

The boob shining white. No lights from any of the buildings. Only the sound of Olive singing to herself, 'You are my sunshine, my only sunshine'.}

{SCENE 42   INT. THE DORMITORY. NIGHT.

Molly and Gracie are whispering together. Daisy sleeps.

MOLLY: This place funny. Funny trees. White land. I don't like it.}

{SCENE 43 EXT. THE RABBIT-PROOF FENCE. NIGHT.

The fence running through the night landscape of the desert, like a dream.}

SCENE 44   INT./EXT. THE DORMITORY. MORNING.   {56*}

(Note: in the finished film Scenes 54 and 55 are a montage of Molly's dreams as she sleeps in the dormitory: Moodoo staring at her as he rides past; Neville bending down to look at her; Riggs reaching out to her; Miss Jessop. As she dreams she speaks: 'This place make me sick ... these people ...sick ... Make me sick.' She wakes, and there is a flashback of the eagle circling overhead, watched by Maude and Molly. The following scene begins with Nina telling everyone to 'Come on and make your beds. Nice and tidy. If you've already done it, get to the church now. Hurry up. Stop dawdling'.) Molly is folding her blanket. Around her girls are getting ready for church. Big girls are doing little girls' hair, the little girls squealing and complaining. One big girl is trying to drag a little girl out from under her bed.

The church bell begins to toll. Nina shouts over to Molly.

NINA: Hey {you.} Molly. You empty the bucket.

> *(Note: in the finished film Nina adds 'then the three of you go to the church'.) Molly looks at her, says nothing. Everyone is hurrying out.* {Nina pauses at the door.

You better hurry up. You be late for church.}

> *Molly says nothing. The church bell is tolling. Molly goes to the door. Looks out.*

{SCENE 45 EXT. MOORE RIVER NATIVE SETTLEMENT. MORNING.

A few stragglers are making their way up the slope to the church. The sky is overcast.}

SCENE 46   INT./EXT. THE DORMITORY. MORNING.   {56*}

Molly looks up at the sky. There are clouds. She makes an instant decision, turns to Gracie. (Note: in the finished film Molly instructs Grace 'Come on, get your things. We're going'.)
{MOLLY: Get the bucket.
GRACIE: I'm not gunna empty that bucket.

> *Molly looks at her, hard.*

MOLLY: We gunna empty that bucket. And then we goin'.}
GRACIE: Where we goin'?

MOLLY: Home. To mother.

She pulls Daisy off the bed. Daisy looks up at her, unbelieving.

DAISY: How we gunna get home?

Molly is collecting their things, stuffing the combs, mirrors in Daisy's bag.

MOLLY: {We gunna} walk.

The church bell is still tolling. Molly slings Daisy's bag around her neck. Gracie sits down, plop, on the bed.

GRACIE: We not goin', are we Daisy?

(Note: in the finished film Gracie adds 'We like it here'.) Daisy looks at Molly, nods. Molly is getting the bucket.

DAISY: That tracker. He put us in that boob.

(Note: in the finished film Molly replies 'He's not going to get us and put us in the boob. We just keep walking'.)

MOLLY: It gunna rain. We gotta go now.

The bell has stopped tolling. Molly grabs Daisy, pulls her toward the door. She has the bucket. Daisy looks up at her.

{DAISY: Ken we take our dresses?

Molly nods.}

GRACIE: It too far, Molly.

She sits there on the bed, empty bag in her hand. Molly checks outside, looks desperately at Gracie, hisses at her.

MOLLY: Come Gracie. Now.

Looks outside again.

{SCENE 47 EXT. MOORE RIVER NATIVE SETTLEMENT. MORNING.

The path is empty.}

{SCENE 48 INT. THE DORMITORY. MORNING.

Gracie is swinging her legs. Molly stands at the door, bucket in one hand, Daisy clasped by the wrist in the other.

MOLLY: We goin' home, Gracie. Get your shoes.

She steps out the door and down the steps. She does not look to see if Gracie is following.

Gracie sits on the bed, bag in one hand. Looks around the empty room. Makes a decision. She pushes herself off the bed. Grabs her shoes from underneath the bed. One furtive look out the door.}

SCENE 49 INT. THE CHURCH. MORNING.   {57*}

Moodoo stands alone at the back of the church, the doors open behind him. Tracy is standing in front of him.

Children and adults are singing a hymn. 'All things bright and beautiful ...'

SCENE 50 EXT. MOORE RIVER NATIVE SETTLEMENT. MORNING.   {58}

Molly is walking briskly across the main path towards the latrines, Daisy stumbling along beside her.

Gracie runs to catch up with Molly and Daisy.

SCENE 51 EXT. MOORE RIVER NATIVE SETTLEMENT. MORNING.   {57*}

The church doors are open. The sound of the hymn comes to them. They reach the middle of the path. '... All creatures great and small ...'

{The slops in the bucket slosh around, threaten to spill.}

SCENE 52 EXT. MOORE RIVER NATIVE SETTLEMENT – THE LATRINES. MORNING.   {59}

'... All things wise and wonderful, the Lord God made them all' as they reach the latrines. Molly drops Daisy's wrist, pushes open the door. Empties the bucket into the long drop. Daisy stands, hands over her mouth and nose. Gracie arrives, stands with Daisy. Molly makes no comment. She drops the bucket to the rear of the latrines, looks over the valley, across to the north.

MOLLY: We goin'. Run.

She doesn't leave them any time for arguing. Doesn't look back. Sets off away from the Settlement, dodging bushes, leaping, skidding. Sliding. She can hear the others following.

The faint sound of another hymn starting up.

SCENE 53 INT. THE DORMITORY. LATE AFTERNOON. {60}

Girls everywhere, sitting on beds in groups of two and three. Miss Jessop conducts the roll call, standing near the door.

MISS JESSOP: Irene Clark.

NANCY: Here, {Miss.}

{MISS JESSOP: May Jones.

ELLIE: Here, Miss.}

> *(Note: in the finished film Miss Jessop calls Ellie Moodoo, and Tracy replies 'Here'.)*

MISS JESSOP: Molly Craig.

Silence.

[*Louder*] Molly Craig.

She looks up, around the group. The girls look all around, at each other.

[*Louder still*] Molly Craig.

The silence grows. Miss Jessop looks at her sheet, draws in a breath.

Gracie Fields.

Silence.

Daisy Kadibil.

Silence. Miss Jessop purses her lips. Looks all around.

Nina, have you seen the new girls?

NINA: {No, Miss. They weren't at church, Miss.}

The girls are abuzz. They shout out, laugh, jeer.

We ain't seen 'em all day, Miss.

SCENE 54 EXT. MOODOO'S SHANTY. LATE AFTERNOON. {61}

A bower shelter, tent shape, made of branches and old sacks. In the distance, other shelters.

Moodoo and an old Aboriginal man sit around a campfire outside. The old man is playing a mouth organ.

A boy, Billy, eight, pants from running. He's dressed in Moore River clothes.

BILLY: You better come quick.

SCENE 55 EXT. THICKLY WOODED HILLS. DAY.   {62}

The figures of the three girls – Molly out in front, leading, steady, dogged. Behind her, some distance away, Gracie, stumbling, struggling, and behind her the tiny figure of Daisy, her head down, shoulders drooping with exhaustion.

SCENE 56 EXT. MOORE RIVER NATIVE SETTLEMENT – THE LATRINES. DAY.   {63}

Moodoo stands at the back of the latrines. He holds his horse's reins, looks at the footprints of the girls.

SCENE 57 EXT. THICKLY WOODED HILLS. LATE AFTERNOON.   {64, 66}

Molly looks back at her tracks. Behind her Gracie and Daisy are spread out. She looks at the sky. Still no rain.

SCENE 58 EXT. THICKLY WOODED HILLS. LATE AFTERNOON.   {65}

Moodoo leans from the side of his horse, looking at the ground. The horse picks its way delicately through the scrub. Moodoo digs his heels into his horse, lets it have its head as it picks its way easily across the ground.

He stops at a bush, looks across the low land, sees where they have gone. Looks up at the sky. Digs his heels in again. The horse responds.

SCENE 59 EXT. THICKLY WOODED HILLS. DUSK.   {68}

{*Molly presses on, skirting the bushes, heading for some low-lying hills in the distance. Every now and then she looks up at the sky. Gracie and Daisy trail behind her. Molly stops near a bush for them to catch up. Gracie arrives, dragging her feet. They wait for Daisy.*

A drop of rain.}

Molly feels it. She looks up. The rain {strengthens,} begins in earnest. {Daisy arrives, face wet from the rain.} Molly gives a little smile. {Sets off, the rain streaming down her face.}

SCENE 60 EXT. THICKLY WOODED HILLS. DUSK.   {67}

Heavy rain.

Moodoo is walking, looking at the ground. He holds the reins of his horse. {There is almost no light.

Moodoo stops. Gets down on one knee. The rain runs down his neck, splatters the ground, washing away the tracks as he watches. Moodoo stands, mutters to himself in language, leads his horse over to the shelter of some bushes.}

{SCENE 61 EXT. LOW HILLS. NIGHT.

The faint shapes of, first, Molly, then Gracie and Daisy, move rapidly across some low hills in the dark.}

SCENE 62 EXT. WHITE GUMS. EARLY MORNING.   {70}

{First light. A bare hillside. A few bird calls. Nothing in sight.

And then a movement as Molly turns her head to look up.} Molly and Daisy are lying under the shelter of a tree, {Daisy's bag under her head. Gracie has gone.

The rain has stopped.

Molly looks around for Gracie, worried. Gracie appears. She is holding out a dead rabbit. Laughing. Molly screams at her.

MOLLY: Where you bin? You don't go 'way.

> *Molly snatches the rabbit from her, flings it to the ground. Daisy watches, wide-eyed.*

We got no time. We goin'.

> *Gracie stamps her foot.*

GRACIE: I'm goin' back. We gunna die.

> *Molly is unmoved.*

MOLLY: Nah, we be alright, Gracie. We jest go that way: north.

Gracie puts her arms around Daisy, tries another tack.

GRACIE: Daisy don't want to go, do you Dais?

Daisy looks at Molly.

DAISY: I'm scared that tracker.

Molly looks at them, decides.

MOLLY: Well I'm goin'. You two can come if you want.

She sets off. The others watch her go, Gracie still holding Daisy. She disappears over the hill. They stand there, in the silence, utterly alone.

Daisy slides out of Gracie's arms, takes her hand and begins to follow Molly. Past the dead body of the rabbit, lying on the rain-soaked ground.}

SCENE 63 INT. NEVILLE'S OFFICE. DAY.   {71}

(Note: in the finished film Scene 68 is Molly smiling in the rain, holding Gracie and Daisy under a tree. Scene 69 is an aerial shot of the hills at night.) Mr Neville sits at his desk, {to one side a sandwich laid out on greaseproof paper. He is looking at some photographs.

A knock on the door. Miss Thomas pokes her head in.

MISS THOMAS: I am sorry to interrupt ...

Neville looks up. Holds out one of the photographs for her to see.

NEVILLE: Mrs Neville's and my trip to the far north.

A photograph of a car laden with supplies on a dirt track in the outback. He gives her a wry smile. Looks at the photo again. Says, almost to himself:

Intrepid explorers.

MISS THOMAS: Mr Neal is ringing from Moore River. He insists on speaking to you.

He hands the photograph to her. Neville picks up the phone. Miss Thomas stands looking at the photograph.

Neville.

He listens.

Which girls?

Listens. Looks at Miss Thomas. She goes to leave but he motions for her to stay.

Yes, yes. When were they last seen?

Listens. His mouth sets.} *He is not pleased.*

That's two days ago.

Listens. Says firmly:

I'll need to be kept fully informed on this, Mr Neal.

Puts the phone firmly down. Looks over to Miss Thomas.

Those three girls {we've just had brought in from the desert.} They've run off.

MISS THOMAS: Oh, dear.

{She hands the photo back to him. Neville doesn't look at it. Sits thinking. Says, almost to himself:}

NEVILLE: It'll be the older one.

He looks at her.

I wondered when I saw her ... Too much of their mind ... unfathomable.

He draws himself up straighter in his chair.

The tracker's on to it. In the meantime it must be kept out of the papers.

SCENE 64 EXT. LOW HILLS. DAY.   {72}

Molly is resting beside a bush. Gracie arrives, flops down beside her. Daisy appears, sits close to Molly, hugging her legs tight into her chest.

{DAISY: We lost.

MOLLY: Nah, we not lost. We keep goin' that way.

She gestures north.

Gracie is pulling leaves off the bush, throwing them down.} *She looks up at the sky.*

GRACIE: No more rain. Tracker gunna get us {now}.

MOLLY: No, he don't.

She pushes herself off the ground. Starts off again. The others follow, Gracie mumbling to herself.

SCENE 65 EXT. WHITE GUMS. DAY.   {73}

David Moodoo is standing in front of the girls' sleeping place, the reins of his horse in one hand. {He is holding the dead rabbit, twisting it, it's head flopping from side to side, glassy eyes staring.}

SCENE 66 EXT. A SMALL RIVER. AFTERNOON.   {74}

Molly, Gracie and Daisy stand on the bank of a river, their bags slung around their necks. They're wearing their shoes.

Molly looks across to the bank. Looks up the river. Looks down it. She watches as a small branch is buffeted along the bank and is carried away. She makes a decision.

MOLLY: Daisy, give me your bag.

> *Daisy holds tight onto the bag. Molly makes a grab for it. Daisy twists away from her.*

Give it here, Daisy.

> {*She wrenches it off her shoulder.*

DAISY: My bag. My bag.

> *Molly hisses at them.*

MOLLY: Wait here.}

> *She steps into the water and begins to wade upstream. {Daisy follows, calling after her.*

DAISY: My things, my things.}

> *Molly stops. {Takes out the little mirror and comb. Puts them in her bag. She sets off again upstream. Gracie and Daisy stand calf-deep in the river and watch as she wades upstream.} She stops some way off and lodges the bag in the roots of some trees close to the bank. Then she turns and begins to wade back. (Note: in the finished film Molly tells Gracie and Daisy 'Hurry up, in the water — in the water!')*

SCENE 67 EXT. NEAR THE SMALL RIVER. AFTERNOON.   {75}

Moodoo on horseback. He sits easy in the saddle. He can see the tracks clearly. Ahead is the river and the tracks leading to it.

SCENE 68 EXT. THE SMALL RIVER. AFTERNOON.   {76}

Molly, Gracie and Daisy are wading calf-deep through the water downstream. The water surges along. It knocks up against their legs, swirling grass and debris along with it. Every now and then Molly looks anxiously back along the bank. Gracie and Daisy struggle behind her.

Laura Monaghan as Gracie, Tianna Sansbury as Daisy and Everlyn Sampi as Molly.

SCENE 69 EXT. THE SMALL RIVER. AFTERNOON.   {77}

Moodoo sits on his horse looking along the river bank. Watches the debris being carried along. He is unhurried. Looks across the river. Looks upstream. Looks downstream. Looks upstream. Now he's seen something. Turns his horse and begins riding along the bank upstream, picking his way carefully on the horse. He stops at the bag. Looks down at it. Looks further upstream. Urges the horse forward.

SCENE 70 EXT. THE SMALL RIVER. AFTERNOON.   {78}

Molly, Gracie and Daisy wade downstream, Molly leading.

SCENE 71 EXT. THE SMALL RIVER. AFTERNOON.   {79}

Moodoo on his horse, stopped. He looks around. Looks carefully downstream. **{***Turns the horse. Sets off back downstream.***}**

SCENE 72 EXT. THE SMALL RIVER. AFTERNOON.   {80, 82}

Molly, Gracie and Daisy push downstream. Ahead, some tall grasses grow right down the bank and into the water.

Molly can hear something. She stops. Gestures violently to Gracie to be quiet. All three girls stand in the water, listening.

The sound of horses hooves, intermittent, walking in the distance. The horse is coming towards them.

Daisy holds tight to Gracie, begins to whimper. Gracie looks wildly at Molly. Molly is desperately looking around. **{***She sees the grass. The hooves are coming closer, more solid now, walking faster. Molly pulls them towards the grass. Gracie and Daisy are whimpering in terror.***}**

SCENE 73 EXT. THE SMALL RIVER. AFTERNOON.   {81}

Moodoo rides on his horse, eyes scouring the river bank for tracks, then sweeping out across the water.

{SCENE 74 EXT. THE SMALL RIVER. AFTERNOON.

Molly, Gracie and Daisy huddle together, crouching in the tall grass. Molly reaches out an arm and pulls the grass straight around them. They can hear the hooves almost upon them.}

SCENE 75 EXT. THE SMALL RIVER. AFTERNOON.   {83}

Moodoo rides faster now. He gives the horse a kick, urges it forward. Something is troubling him. As he passes, pull focus to see the girls hidden in the foreground. The sound of Moodoo's horse in the water grows fainter as he continues downstream.

{SCENE 76 EXT. LOW HILLS. NIGHT.

Molly, Gracie and Daisy are curled up asleep under the shelter of a bush.}

SCENE 77 EXT. LOW HILLS. DAY.   {84}

(Note: in the finished film this scene begins with Molly pretending that she can see an emu, and a kangaroo, for them to eat. Gracie replies that 'We don't know this place. How we going to eat?'. When the hunters appear, the girls hide, but Gracie convinces Molly to ask them for something to eat.) Next day. Molly walks along a cattle track. She ducks behind a tree, signals to Gracie and Daisy behind her. She has seen something in the distance. Gracie and Daisy creep up to stand behind her. They peer out.

Something moving. It comes closer.

They wait.

Two Aboriginal hunters, bare feet, trousers and shirts, walk towards them. One has a cooked kangaroo slung around his neck. Daisy pulls on Molly's dress. Molly hisses at her.

MOLLY: Wait.

> *The two men come nearer. Molly steps out. The men see her, stop. Molly twists her hand, signals to them.*

> [*Signalling*] What's up?

> *One of the men signals back, repeating the sign, reassuring. Molly walks towards the hunters, Gracie and Daisy follow, pushing up against her in their eagerness. They meet in the track.*

FIRST HUNTER: Where you girls from? You from that Moore River?

Molly nods. Daisy dances about.

DAISY: We walking home … {all the way.}

FIRST HUNTER: Where your country?

MOLLY: {We from} Jigalong.

FIRST HUNTER: {That too far.} Long way. {[*To the second hunter*] Matches.}

    The second hunter feels in his pockets. Gives Molly a packet of matches.

You know what you doing?

    Molly nods. The first hunter slides the kangaroo to the ground, takes out a knife and slices off the tail.

That tracker from Moore River. He pretty good {one. You watch out.}

    (Note: in the finished film the Hunter adds 'I heard he get them runaways all the time. Got to be good to beat him. Take you back to that place. You watch out for him, eh?') He hands the tail to Molly, hoists the kangaroo back around his neck and walks off with the second hunter.

SCENE 78 EXT. LOW HILLS. AFTERNOON.   {85}

Molly tears pieces of meat off the kangaroo and they squat, chewing. Gracie throws the bones aside.

GRACIE: You think you're so clever. Where are we?

    She spreads her hands out. Looks all around.

We lost.

    Molly stands. She looks all around. Figures north. Points.

MOLLY: Jigalong that way. North.

{SCENE 79 EXT. SCRUB COUNTRY. DAY.

An enormous paddock, flat and bare. A few trees, a broken down fence. Three tiny specks in the distance.}

{SCENE 80 EXT. SCRUB COUNTRY. DAY.

Molly is digging. Gracie and Daisy lie exhausted, watching her. She digs out some roots of a plant, wipes them on her skirt and hands them over. Digs again. Gets more and starts walking, chewing on the root. Gracie and Daisy wearily follow.}

SCENE 81 INT. NEVILLE'S OFFICE. DAY.   {86}

Neville and Sellenger are standing at Neville's desk, studying a map.

NEVILLE: {Moore River.}

>   *He points and traces their route.*

The tracker followed them to this riverbank and then lost them completely. About a week ago. There's been no sign of them since.

>   *He looks up at Sellenger. Sellenger moves the map a little, bends over it to study it. Straightens. He looks at Neville. (Note: in the finished film Sellenger asks 'Three little half-castes?'.)*

SELLENGER: We're talking quite a few man hours here. Who's going to pay for it?

>   *Neville moves the map back.*

NEVILLE: There's very little money in my departmental budget.

>   *He looks at Sellenger.*

I'm hoping that if your men can in some way combine it with their regular duties …

SELLENGER: We'll be able to handle all the notifications, posting all the police stations, farms et cetera …

>   *Neville interrupts him.*

NEVILLE: We'll provide a description, of course.

>   *Sellenger ignores the interruption.*

SELLENGER: … But if my men are making trips outside of their duties then I'm afraid it will be an impost on your department, Mr Neville.

NEVILLE: If your men are out on other jobs at the same time, Inspector, there would be no extra expense.

SELLENGER: I'll concede that, Mr Neville.

NEVILLE: And it is the job of every one of your men, in their role as local protectors.

SELLENGER: My men will all do their jobs, Mr Neville.

>   *Sellenger turns back to the map.*

Now, a week ago, you say.

{SCENE 82 EXT. THE TAPLINS' FARMHOUSE HILL. DAY.

A hill looking down on the front of a farmer's house. Smoke comes from the chimney. A hen house and run and a large shed stand in the yard.

An old man sits in a chair reading a newspaper, one leg stuck out before him. A little girl, Em, eight, is playing under a table. Two men are sawing wood in the paddock beyond the house. The sound of the saw drifts over.}

SCENE 83 EXT. THE TAPLIN'S FARMHOUSE. DAY.   {88}

Molly runs across the open space to the hen-house door. She pulls the bolt and slips inside. It's dark and dry.

SCENE 84 INT. THE HEN HOUSE. DAY.   {89}

Some hens on roosts look at Molly. Two are on nests in boxes. Some dirty old crusts of bread lie on the ground. Molly stuffs one in her mouth, the other in her pocket.

She goes over to a sitting hen, feels under her. The hen turns its head, looks at her, rearranges itself as she withdraws an egg.

Then the door abruptly opens, spilling the light in. Molly jumps. A large figure is standing there.

MRS TAPLIN: And what d'you think you might be up to? Thieving my eggs, eh? Come out here where I can see you. And get rid of that bread. It's filthy.

Molly takes some of the bread out of her mouth.

Now, come on out here. Come on. I'm not going to bite you.

Mrs Taplin, 35, thin, sharp eyes but not an unkind face, bare legs under the apron and thin dress.

SCENE 85 EXT. THE TAPLIN'S FARMHOUSE – THE HEN HOUSE. DAY.   {90}

Mrs Taplin steps back to let Molly out, then pulls the door firmly shut and bolts it.

MRS TAPLIN: You on ya own? Got anyone with you?

Molly looks at her. Makes a decision. She looks over towards Gracie and Daisy.

{Call them over, then. Go on.

Molly gives a whistle and signals.

[*To Molly*] I'll take that.

Molly hands her the egg.}

Hungry, eh? You want somethin' to eat, you should ask.

SCENE 86 EXT. THE TAPLINS' FARMHOUSE. DAY.   {91*}

Mrs Taplin brings out a tray with a plate of food: thick slices of bread and cold meat, six mugs of tea. Puts it on the table. She hands a cup to the old man.

MRS TAPLIN: Here you are, father. You keep your stick to yourself.

> *The old man puts his newspaper down beside his chair. Puts his stick on top of it. A report on the missing girls is headlined on the page. He takes his cup. Em takes a cup, holding it carefully, sipping. She hands the tray down to the girls standing at the foot of the steps.*

Where you girls planning on going?

{*Molly swallows.*

MOLLY: Home.

MRS TAPLIN: Home. And where might that be?}

> *Molly says nothing. Takes another bite.*

Cat got your tongue, eh?

> *She has another look at Daisy, who is shivering.*

SCENE 87 EXT. THE TAPLINS' FARMHOUSE – THE SHED. DAY.
{91*}

The sawing has stopped and the men are moving towards the house. Molly is wearing an old army greatcoat. Gracie and Daisy struggle into smaller jackets. They are drowned in them. Mrs Taplin has seen the men. They are much closer.

MRS TAPLIN: Now, get.

> *Molly begins to walk away. Mrs Taplin calls after them.*

And watch out for those boys further along.

> *She waves an arm, off to the right, indicating the direction.*

They go out rabbitin' along the fence.

> *Molly stops. Turns. Looks at her.*

MOLLY: That rabbit fence?

> *Mrs Taplin nods.*

MRS TAPLIN: Yes, that rabbit fence.

MOLLY: Where that fence?

> *Mrs Taplin nods east, warning them.*

MRS TAPLIN: East. {A few miles. Be careful.}

Molly leads them away from the approaching men, across the field. North.

{*The two men stand on the verandah taking off their gumboots and looking after them. The old man points after them with his stick.*

They reach a bend in the road and Molly looks back. Em is standing alone at the shed, looking after them.}

{SCENE 88 INT./EXT. NEVILLE'S HOME. AFTERNOON.

Through the window in Neville's front room we see Peter, eight, Neville's son, running up the path towards the house.

As he runs from view around the side of the house the camera swings with him to reveal Alice, twenty-two, Neville's maid bending to reach for some china teacups in a glass-fronted china cabinet against the wall. On top of the cabinet some framed photos: a wedding photo and photos of Neville in the far north on expedition.

She stands and places the cups carefully on top of the cabinet. Beside her, a door. The door opens and Peter bursts in. He's waving a telegram. He runs to two closed doors in the far wall, flings them open. Stands there.

Mrs Neville is standing behind Neville, her arms around him. He holds a golf putter and she stands close to him, her hands on his hands. For a moment they are oblivious to the interruption. Then they sense his presence. They look over to Peter. Laugh. She steps away from him.

Peter holds up the envelope.

PETER: A telegram for you, Daddy.

> *He walks over to Neville, the telegram held high. Mrs Neville joins him, linking her arm through his. Neville reads the telegram. Says to his wife:*

NEVILLE: Good news. They've found those three little girls I was telling you about.

> *She smiles at him, pats his arm. Neville turns to Peter.*

Run and tell the boy there's a reply.}

{SCENE 89 INT./EXT. A POLICE CAR – THE ROAD TO THE TAPLINS' FARM. DAY

A telegram on the passenger seat of a police car. Constable Brett is driving. The car is making its way along a country road on its way to the Taplin farm. }

{SCENE 90 EXT. THE TAPLINS' FARMHOUSE ROAD. DAY.

Mrs Taplin stands on the verandah at the back door looking across the field. The police car is pulled up on the road. Constable Brett is kneeling, talking with Em. As she watches, Em points across the field in the direction taken by the girls.}

SCENE 91 EXT. SCRUBBY HILLS. DAY. {92}

Molly, Gracie and Daisy are walking, chewing on bread as they go. They are strung out, Molly in the lead.

As Molly walks she looks up ahead, then back to where they've come from. She then deliberately changes direction. Keeps walking. Gracie runs to catch up with her. She indicates over to where they've come from, a lump of bread in her hand. (Note: in the finished film Gracie asks 'Which way now?'.)

{GRACIE: We went that way. And now we goin' back, other way.

Daisy arrives. She looks up at Molly, doubting.

DAISY: Where we goin'?**}**
MOLLY: That rabbit fence.

She leans in to Daisy, eyes sparkling.

It here.

She looks back to Gracie.

We find it. We kin folla it home.

(Note: in the finished film Daisy adds 'And we see our mum'.)

SCENE 92 INT. DORMITORY. NIGHT. {94}

(Note: in the finished film Scene 93 is the girls walking across a desert plain.) Girls in the dormitory, some warming themselves around two little fires in kerosene tins, others two or three to a bed, all listening to Nina read from a scrap of a newspaper. (Note: in the finished film Nina reads 'The Chief Protector of Aborigines, Mr A.O. Neville, is concerned about three native girls, ranging from eight to fourteen years of age, who a month ago ran away from the Moore River Native Settlement. He would be grateful if any person who saw them would notify him promptly.')

NINA: 'We have been searching high and low for the children for a week past and all the trace we found of them was a dead rabbit', Mr Devil said.

(Note: in the finished film they have been 'searching for a month'.) The girls hoot and laugh, {shout 'Dead rabbit'. Nina holds the scrap of paper up. Waves for everyone to be quiet. Becomes very serious.

'We are very anxious that no harm may come to them in the bush.'

More hooting and laughing.}

{SCENE 93 EXT. SCRUBBY HILLS. NIGHT.

The three girls sleep huddled together, wrapped in Molly's army jacket. A few branches have been broken into a bower.}

{SCENE 94 EXT. SCRUBBY HILLS. DAY.

The girls walk, a little strung out. Molly is scanning the country ahead. She can see a hill protruding a little way off.}

{SCENE 95 EXT. A LOOKOUT. DAY.

The girls on top of the hill. A vast panorama stretches out before them. No fence anywhere in sight. Gracie and Daisy are too exhausted to respond. Molly looks east.

MOLLY: That way.

She sets off.}

SCENE 96 EXT. THE RABBIT-PROOF FENCE – JIGALONG. DAY.
{87}

(Note: in the finished film the following scene takes place at the Jigalong depot.) {Maude and Frinda walk in the bush near the fence.

Reg walks up the fence carrying some rolled netting on his shoulder. He sees them, lowers the netting to the ground, waves them over. Maude goes over. Frinda stands back. Reg leans on his shovel.}

REG: Your girls have gone.

Maude doesn't understand.

MAUDE: Eh? What you say?

REG: They've run away from that Moore River. Gone.

Maude looks at him. Says nothing. Turns and begins to walk back to Frinda.

[Shouting after her] Everyone's looking for 'em.

She stands a little straighter, her face lightened.

{SCENE 97 EXT. SCRUBBY HILLS. DAY.

The girls walk. Molly looks far ahead, her eyes scouring the countryside.}

SCENE 98 EXT. SCRUBBY HILLS. DAY.   {95*}

Molly walks ahead of Gracie and Daisy. She walks easily, economically, picking her way through the undergrowth, around bushes. As she walks she scans the country ahead, and then a glint. She keeps walking, quickening her pace, begins to push impatiently through the grass bushes. The object appears more and more solid, more and more there. She turns, signals to the others. Whistles. (Note: in the finished film Daisy calls 'It's the fence. It's the fence. She found it!'.)

SCENE 99 EXT. THE RABBIT-PROOF FENCE – SCRUBBY HILLS. DAY.   {95*, 97, 99}

Molly runs, breaks through to the cleared area around the fence. Stops there. Looks down along the fence. It goes for as far as she can see. Looks up the fence. It goes right to the horizon in the other direction. Gracie and Daisy come out of the scrub and stand beside her. Silence. Molly takes the few steps to the fence. She grabs the top wire and stands there, holding it, turned to the north, towards her country.

{MOLLY: Now we get home.}

SCENE 100 EXT. THE RABBIT-PROOF FENCE – JIGALONG. DAY.   {96, 98, 100}

Maude stands on her own near the fence. One hand rests lightly on the wire. She is looking south along the fence. (Note: in the finished film Scenes 97-100 cut between Maude and the girls, linked by the fence.)

SCENE 101 INT. NEVILLE'S OFFICE. AFTERNOON.   {101}

A large map of the whole of Western Australia covers Neville's desk. Neville and Detective Inspector Sellenger are standing, looking at it. Sellenger reads from a copy of a police report.

{SELLENGER: Seven days ago they were east of Dalwillinu.

He and Neville bend over the map and Sellenger places his index finger on the spot.

Here it is.

NEVILLE: It should have been a simple-enough undertaking.

Sellenger turns his head to look at him, but holds his finger on the map.

SELLENGER: My man did his best, Mr Neville. Accounts for the car hire and travelling are attached to his report. I'll leave it with you.

He bends over the map once more, moves it so that he can see it properly. }

Now, this latest sighting, which is four days old, {had them about here, around Yalgoo.

He taps the map with his finger.

A knock on the door.} Miss Thomas comes in. She speaks quietly to Neville.

MISS THOMAS: The man from the newspaper –

NEVILLE: I have nothing more to say to him.

Miss Thomas leaves. Neville edges around so that he can see.

Let me see. Bunnawarra ...

He traces the route on the map.

... Yalgoo.

He flattens the map with his left hand, extends the route with his right.

They're on the fence. They're following the fence.

He edges back to allow Sellenger to see, keeping his hands on the map. Sellenger moves in closer. Works it out. Turns to look at Neville.

SELLENGER: You're right.

Neville smiles.

NEVILLE: Just because a people use Neolithic tools, Inspector, it does not mean they have Neolithic minds.

He turns back to the map.

So that makes the task very much easier. Look here. There's a branch off to the west, just north of Yalgoo.

He runs his finger up the fence, shows the junction. Sellenger looks closely.

{SELLENGER: Yes, that's right.

Neville spreads out the map with both hands, holds it flat, leans on them to look up at Sellenger.}

NEVILLE: You get your man out to that fence north of the junction. He can start coming down it after them. I'll have Moodoo coming up from the south to meet them.

Brings his hands together. Clasps them.

We can't miss them.

SCENE 102 EXT. THE RABBIT-PROOF FENCE – SCRUBBY HILLS. DAY.   {104, 105}

Molly and Gracie walk along the cleared ground beside the rabbit-proof fence. There is no sign of Daisy.

MOLLY: Wait here, {Gracie.}

Gracie walks over into the scrub. Slumps to the ground. Molly turns and goes back along the fence. Daisy is favouring one leg, holding onto a fence post.

DAISY: I can't walk no more, Molly. Me leg.

She holds out her leg. It is covered in weeping sores. Molly gives it a cursory glance.

{MOLLY: You alright.

DAISY: It hurts.}

MOLLY: I'm not carryin' ya far, Daisy. {Ya too heavy.}

She bends to let Daisy climb on her back.

SCENE 103 EXT. THE RABBIT-PROOF FENCE – FLAT COUNTRY. AFTERNOON.   {102}

A police car edges its way south down the fence. Constable Brett is driving.

SCENE 104 EXT. THE RABBIT-PROOF FENCE – SCRUBBY HILLS. AFTERNOON.   {103}

Moodoo, on his horse, makes his way north along the fence.

{SCENE 105 EXT. THE RABBIT-PROOF FENCE – A JUNCTION. AFTERNOON.

Molly squats with Gracie and Daisy, hidden in the scrub. Ahead of them the fence splits.

The fence beyond the junction takes on a different character. The land is now rocky and these fences do not run straight but bend around outcrops. Nor are they as well cleared on either side.

GRACIE: Which way?

Molly is carefully considering. She looks in both directions. Gestures to the left. Gracie looks to the right. Looks to the left. Says nothing.

MOLLY: We go?

She sets off, keeping to the edge of the cleared ground. Gracie and Daisy trudge after her.}

SCENE 106 EXT. THE RABBIT-PROOF FENCE – SCRUBBY HILLS. AFTERNOON.   {108}

(Note: in the finished film Scene 106 is the police driving along the fence. Scene 107 is Moodoo riding along the fence. This scene begins with Molly carrying Daisy, saying 'Don't think I'm carrying you all the way'.) The girls walk along the fence. Ahead of them smoke from a small fire rises into the still air. **{Daisy is limping, exhausted. She tugs on Molly's dress.}**

DAISY: Camp, Molly.

They stop to consider. Daisy sinks to the ground.

{GRACIE: Ask 'im. Just some tea, Molly. It'll be alright.

Molly looks at Daisy. Decides.

MOLLY: C'mon, then, we'll get somethin' to eat.}

SCENE 107 EXT. THE RABBIT-PROOF FENCE – BRIAN'S CAMP. AFTERNOON.   {109}

A tent and a small fire with a billy boiling on it. A man sits with his back to the girls as they approach. He hears them coming and turns. It's a fence worker, Brian Bismarck, a man in his mid-forties, rough, easy going.

BRIAN: Company.

{*He sizes them up, takes them in.*

How many of youse? Three? Come.

He beckons, friendly.

Come on. I'm just about to make some tea. Could do with some company.

He throws some tea in the billy, waits, takes it off the fire with a stick under the handle. The girls edge forward.

You girls hungry? Want some tucker? Come on then.}

SCENE 108 EXT. THE RABBIT-PROOF FENCE – SCRUBBY HILLS. DUSK.   {111}

Moodoo on his horse. Impassive. The horse walks comfortably down the cleared side of the fence.

SCENE 109 EXT. THE RABBIT-PROOF FENCE – BRIAN'S CAMP. DUSK.   {110}

The campfire burns. The girls sit comfortably, relaxed, around it. Daisy is asleep against Molly.

BRIAN: Where you girls heading?

Molly is drawing in the sand, not looking at him, careful. She doesn't say anything.

You going to Mullewa? Your family's there?

Molly looks at him, guarded.

MOLLY: Where {that place …} Mullewa?

Brian pokes the fire, resettles the billy. Nods along the fence.

BRIAN: That way, west. Further along the number-two.

Molly looks up at him, startled.

MOLLY: There more than one rabbit fence?

He laughs, waves with his stick in all directions.

BRIAN: My oath {there are}.

(Note: in the finished film Brian adds 'We've got three of them'.) Gracie whispers to Molly.

GRACIE: We on the wrong fence.

Molly looks up the fence line, looks directly at him.

MOLLY: How we find that number-one fence?
BRIAN: That way.

He indicates with his head.

Over that way. Where you come from.

Gracie groans. Brian looks at her, looks at Daisy sleeping.

You could cut across. Look.

He takes a stick, draws a large 'Y' shape in the sand.

You're here. See?

Molly looks. He taps on the left of the 'Y'.

But you wanna be here.

He taps on the right branch of the 'Y'.

So if you cut across here.

He draws a line across.

It'll save ya twenty, thirty mile. It's not hard.

(Note: in the finished film they would save themselves 'a hundred miles or so'.)
Molly is already standing, ready to go.

{You better rest a bit here.

He nods at Daisy.

Let her sleep. You can go in the morning.}

{SCENE 110 EXT. THE RABBIT-PROOF FENCE – BRIAN'S CAMP.
DAWN.

It is the early hours of the morning, first dawn.

Molly shakes Daisy awake. Gracie stands, half asleep, beside her. Molly takes Daisy by the hand, leads her off. Gracie follows.

They set off north-east, away from the fence, heading up from the tiny hint of light on the horizon.}

SCENE 111 EXT. THE RABBIT-PROOF FENCE – THE JUNCTION.
MORNING.   {112}

The police car is parked at the junction. Brett stands at the open door, ready to get in. Moodoo {holds his horse's reins. He} is {standing} on the other side of the fence.

BRETT: I don't have the petrol. {You going to go back?}

Moodoo {mounts the horse, sits in the saddle. He waves with one hand to the north. Turns the horse into the scrub and} begins to pick his way through the scrubby bushes.

SCENE 112 EXT. THE EVANS' HOMESTEAD. DAY.   {113}

Molly, Gracie and Daisy crouch behind some bushes watching the back of a farmhouse. At the back of the house and separate to it is a washhouse, lavatory and small lean-to room. One long washing line laden with washing stretches across the back yard. An Aboriginal girl, Mavis Short, is at the line, taking in the washing, piling it in a basket.

Molly gives a low whistle. Mavis looks out towards them. Molly whistles again. Mavis looks to the house, comes towards them, stops and looks out. Molly pokes her head up, calls out.

MOLLY: {Hey. We} over here.

Daisy pops her head up.

DAISY: An' we hungry.

Mavis sees them. She looks back to the house, walks towards them, squats down beside them.

MAVIS: Youse that lot from Moore River?

Molly nods.

You girls walk all the way?

(Note: in the finished film she adds '800 miles?'.) Molly nods.

I was there. {Always} too scared to run away, but. Everyone was always caught. Stuck in that boob. You got the furtherest. {You got a long way, eh?} Where you heading?

A voice calls from inside the house.

MRS EVANS: [*out of view*] Mavis, {Mavis. I know you're out there.}

Mavis shouts back to the house.

MAVIS: I'm just getting the washing, Mrs Evans.

She leans towards Molly.

Stay here. I'll come and get you. You can sleep with me tonight. I'll get you some food.

She goes back to the line, picks up the basket, takes it inside the house. Molly looks at the house, looks at Gracie and Daisy, makes a snap decision.

{MOLLY: Wait here.}

Deborah Mailman as Mavis.

She scuttles over to the washing line. Pulls two socks off the line and is back, panting. Grinning. Displaying the socks to the others. She shoves them into Gracie's bag, throws the wooden pegs into the scrub.

SCENE 113 INT. THE EVANS' HOMESTEAD – MAVIS' ROOM. NIGHT.   {116, 118}

(Note: in the finished film Scene 114 is Molly, Daisy and Gracie eating and Scene 115 shows the farm buildings at night. Scene 117 shows Mr Evans' feet walking across dirt.) A tiny windowless room with a narrow bed. {*Molly and Daisy are sleeping on a coat on the floor. Gracie is curled up asleep next to Mavis in her bed.*}

The door slowly edges open. Molly is immediately awake. She sits bolt upright. Daisy stirs and wakens. A large figure edges into the room, easing the door shut behind him. The man fumbles with his trousers. He lifts the blanket off {*Mavis*} *and is about to climb into the bed when he sees Gracie* {*lying beside Mavis. Mavis wakes, tightens her arm around Gracie.*} *(Note: in the finished film Mavis is not present in the room. Mr Evans sees the girls under the blanket, picks up his clothes and leaves. Mavis encounters him just outside and tells Mr Evans 'Go away!', as Molly hurries the girls to wake up so they can leave.)*

{MAVIS: [*in a low voice*] You better get out of here, Mr Evans.

Mr Evans stands there, looking at the two girls.

You better go, Mr Evans.}

He backs to the door, pulling up his trousers. Takes in Molly and Daisy, feels behind him for the door latch, opens it and leaves.

{MOLLY: Mavis, Mavis.

Mavis lifts her head, looks at Molly.

Who that?

MAVIS: That's the boss.

She shudders. Daisy mumbles, half asleep.

DAISY: Big balls.

Mavis flops her head back on the pillow trying not to laugh. Molly hugs Daisy, burying her head in Daisy's neck. They both giggle explosively. Molly recovers.

MOLLY: We better go.

Mavis raises herself on one elbow, careful not to wake Gracie.}

MAVIS: Don't go, Molly. He'll come back if you go. Don't go. He won't say anything.

{MOLLY: We'll stay here a bit longer and then we'll go.}

{SCENE 114 INT. THE EVANS' HOMESTEAD – MAVIS' ROOM.
NIGHT.

Mavis and Gracie sleep in Mavis's bed, Molly and Daisy on the floor.

A car door slams.

Molly wakes with a start. Listens. There are muffled sounds, low voices, the crunching of feet on the gravel. Molly jumps up, shakes Mavis and Gracie.

MOLLY: Gracie, Gracie, get up quick. The p'lice is here. Get your things. Hurry up.

> *She grabs her coat from under Daisy, all the time shaking Daisy violently. Mavis gets Gracie's coat, puts her arms into the sleeves, pulls it onto her shoulders and moves her to the door. Slings her bag around her neck.*

MAVIS: The missus must've rung.

> *Daisy is groggy with sleep and won't wake. Molly whispers urgently in her ear.*

MOLLY: Daisy, Daisy. Come on. Wake up. We goin'.

> *Mavis opens the door. Daisy is still half asleep. Molly scoops her up. Carries her outside.*}

SCENE 115 EXT. THE EVANS' HOMESTEAD – MAVIS' ROOM.
NIGHT.   {125}

(Note: in the finished film Scene 119 shows the farm buildings; Scene 120 shows lights flickering on Mavis' wall; Scene 121 is a car pulling up; Scene 122 is Mavis sitting up in bed; Scene 123 is the policeman walking around the car; in Scene 124 Mavis wakes up the girls and tells them they 'Got to go'.) Gracie keeps as close as she can to Molly.

MAVIS: Run that way and jest keep going.

> *There is no moon and Molly can just make out the shapes of bushes. They run away from Mavis' room, away from the house, {Daisy clinging sleepily onto Molly, her arms around Molly's neck. Molly lets Daisy slip to the ground.*

MOLLY: Daisy, you gotta run now. You wake?

> *She gives her a push.*

Run with Gracie.

Gracie grabs Daisy's hand, pulls her further away.} Molly can see the car in front of the big house, lit up by a lantern. Mavis's room is black in the night. She runs back towards Mavis's room.

The light and footsteps now cross to Mavis's room.

Molly {takes her coat and,} bending, begins to run backwards, sweeping the ground as she does so. {Shouts and the sound of slaps and a cry.} Molly reaches the other two, crouched behind some bushes. She pulls Gracie and Daisy down beside her and they lie stretched out, flat on the ground.

Molly's point of view: Mrs Evans stands at the door of Mavis's room. Mr Evans stands beside her, hands in pockets, scuffing the dirt with his foot. Constable Larsen, holding a lantern aloft, takes a few steps out into the yard, a shadowy figure beside him. The light from a lantern swings around the yard. {Mrs Evans calls to him.}

MRS EVANS: It must be them.

He takes a few steps out. The light beams out just above their heads. The two men stand there.

LARSEN: When did you see them, Mr Evans?

Mr Evans lifts his head.}

MR EVANS: About an hour or so ago. They were running out over there.

Larsen shines the light in a careful arc across the backyard.

Molly lies, head pressed into the earth, frozen with fear. She clutches Gracie and Daisy, pushing them down too.

Larsen and the man walk back to Mrs Evans. Larsen swings the lantern around one more time, Moodoo's black face is caught in the light for a second.

{Molly sees him. Almost cries out in terror. Ducks her head down.}

LARSEN: We'll have to wait for the light to get better. Can't see a thing now.

MRS EVANS: I'll make you a cup of tea.

They turn and go back to the house.

Molly lies there, waiting, heart pounding. She lifts her head a little. Daisy is terrified, can hardly speak.

DAISY: It that tracker.

Molly lifts herself carefully up, pulls Daisy up. Gracie is already crouched. Molly, holding Daisy's arm begins to walk carefully away. Gracie follows. They do not make a sound.

SCENE 116 EXT. SCRUB COUNTRY. FIRST LIGHT.   {126}

Molly, Gracie and Daisy run across country, Molly leading, heading always to the light.

SCENE 117 EXT. THE EVANS' HOMESTEAD. EARLY MORNING.

{128}

(Note: in the finished film Scene 127 is an aerial shot of the girls walking along the fence.) Constable Larsen stands talking to Mrs Evans on the back door step. David Moodoo walks near the clothes line. He has their trail. He moves across the ground, lightly, surely, taking his time. Remorseless. He stoops to retrieve something from the scrub, weighs it in his hand. It's a clothes peg. He pockets it. Now he moves across to the patch where they lay. He gestures, a slight twist of the wrist, an old habit, more to himself than to the others.

SCENE 118 EXT. SCRUBBY, VERY LOW HILLS. EARLY MORNING.   {129}

Molly, Gracie and Daisy sit panting. Molly is putting on the thick men's work socks. They slide down around her ankles. (Note: in the finished film Molly carries Gracie away while Daisy waits in a tree. Molly carefully walks from rock to rock.)

{MOLLY: Gracie, ya hefta wait here.

> *She bends her knees and Daisy clambers onto her back. Molly gives a little shrug so that she is sitting up higher and then she sets off, stepping lightly over the ground. Gracie watches as she disappears over a rise.}*

SCENE 119 EXT. SCRUBBY, VERY LOW HILLS. MORNING. {130}

The country spread out, vast. Moodoo and Larsen walk steadily, not hurrying. As they pass Moodoo indicates each sign with little gestures; the slurred sock marks, the broken grass.

{SCENE 120 EXT. SCRUBBY, VERY LOW HILLS. MORNING.

Silence. Gracie watches the rise, her face puckered anxiously. And then Molly appears. She arrives, grim faced, determined. Gracie clings to her with relief, climbs on her back.}

SCENE 121 EXT. A ROCKY CREEK BED. MORNING.   {131}

The three figures race through the creek bed, Molly leading, as they move rapidly across the ground, jumping from rock to rock, careful not to leave any prints on the ground.

SCENE 122 EXT. THE CREEK BED. DAY.   {132}

Moodoo walks, head bent in concentration, along the creek bed. Larsen walks beside him. They reach the rocks. Moodoo walks across the rocks. Comes to a stop. Stands, looking all around. Turns and walks back. Looks up the bank. Looks around, in a wider arc. Larsen stands waiting for him. Moodoo stands thinking. Starts to walk back through the rocks. (Note: in the finished film the girls hide behind a bush during this scene.)

SCENE 123 INT. NEVILLE'S OFFICE. DAY.   {133}

Neville comes into his office. Sellenger bustles in behind him carrying a large, detailed map. They are arguing.

NEVILLE: I do not expect you to understand what I'm trying to do for these people, but I will not have all my plans put into jeopardy. People don't understand that this problem is not going to just go away. If it is not dealt with now it will fester for years to come.

> *(Note: in the finished film he continues 'These children are that problem. Please explain exactly what happened'.) He sits at his desk, looks at Sellenger who sits down opposite him, the rolled map between his knees. Sellenger unrolls the map.*

SELLENGER: I don't know how they did it but we lost them. I had Larsen out there – Moodoo was with him – and we lost 'em. They're making right fools of us.

NEVILLE: They are indeed, Inspector. And the cost is more than to just our pride. The reputation of this department is beginning to suffer.

> *He looks at him. Sellenger raises an eyebrow. He is laying the map on the desk {over top of several piles of cards, some of which he knocks to the floor.}*

SELLENGER: I can assure you that my men have better things to do than chase your charges all round the country.

> *Sellenger turns to the map, traces the route with a thick finger.*

They're coming up to very rough country. Once they're much past Meekatharra there's no way I can risk any of my men.

{*Neville is picking up the fallen cards. He taps them together.*}

NEVILLE: I agree. We must get them before they get into the real desert country. So, this is what we're going to do.

{*He puts the cards on the edge of the table.*}

We put your man {from Cue} out there, Moodoo can join him. We put them well up the fence, round here.

He taps on the map.

Far enough up so that we know we can't possibly miss them. And I want them to stay there. They can set up camp and wait.

He looks up at Sellenger. Sellenger looks where he's pointing.

SELLENGER: Costly.

NEVILLE: We'll just have to bear it. Their lives may be at stake.

Neville is pondering another possibility. He speaks quietly.

And Inspector, I understand the mother of one of the girls has gone to Wiluna. They're heading into that country. I want the word spread. Let's see what that does.

{*Sellenger refolds the map.*

SELLENGER: We'll get 'em.}

{SCENE 124 EXT. THE RABBIT-PROOF FENCE – FLAT COUNTRY. NIGHT.

The girls walk by the moonlight.}

SCENE 125 EXT. A BICYCLE TRACK – THE RABBIT-PROOF FENCE – FLAT COUNTRY. DAY.   {136}

(Note: in the finished film Scene 135 is an aerial shot of the hills and the desert.) {*Molly, Gracie and Daisy are walking up a rise to the side of the fence. They are playing a game as they walk, throwing pebbles at the fence posts, laughing and cheering as they hit or miss. Molly throws a stone ahead, runs to the top of the rise. Stops.*

Molly's point of view: a man, Dan Willocks, a half-caste stockman, is sitting, leaning against a fence post. There is some bread and meat laid out beside him. He shouts out to her.

DAN: I bin waiting for youse.

He proffers the food. Molly looks at him. Looks at the food. Gracie and Daisy stand beside her.

Come on, get this inta ya. Youse must be starvin'.

He pushes the food towards them, away from him.} They *{walk towards him, fall on the food,}* eat ravenously.

{You girls followin' the fence eh?

Molly nods.

You headin' into real rough country. An' with legs in that state …

He nods at Daisy's legs.

… I don't see how you gunna make it.} Lotta people worried for you. They got p'licemen up and down the country lookin' for youse. It in all the papers.

{MOLLY: We alright. We not goin' back.}

DAN: Which one of youse Gracie?

Molly and Daisy look at Gracie. Dan follows their gaze.

You Gracie?

Gracie looks down at her feet.

I hear your mummy gone to Wiluna. {You know that?}

(Note: in the finished film Dan tells the girls 'You can catch a train there from Meeka'.) Gracie looks at him. Molly pulls Daisy up.

MOLLY: We goin' now.

GRACIE: Wiluna? She at Wiluna?

MOLLY: Come on, Gracie. {We goin' now.

Molly and Daisy are already walking. Gracie looks at Dan, runs after Molly and Daisy. Dan remains sitting there. He calls after them.

DAN: They after you, ya know. They know which way you going. They know you following the fence.}

Gracie walks beside Molly, excited.

{GRACIE: She at Wiluna, Molly. We kin go on the train.}

Molly keeps walking.

MOLLY: {We goin' home, Gracie.} He lyin'.

(Note: in the finished film Gracie replies 'Maybe she there, Molly. Maybe he telling the truth'.) {Gracie has not heard her.

GRACIE: She at Wiluna, Molly. Wiluna.}

{SCENE 126 EXT. THE RABBIT-PROOF FENCE – SCRUBBY
DESERT. DAY.

Walking in the scrub beside the fence.}

{SCENE 127 EXT. SCRUBBY FLAT DESERT. AFTERNOON.

Sleeping a little away from the fence, bracken, spinifex grass.}

{SCENE 128 EXT. RIGGS'S CAMP – LOW HILL COUNTRY.
EVENING.

*Constable Riggs and David Moodoo lie wrapped in blankets. Way in front of them the
fence cuts across the low hills. Beyond, a vast salt lake stretches out to the horizon.*}

{SCENE 129 EXT. THE RABBIT-PROOF FENCE – BARE FLAT
COUNTRY. DAWN.

*Molly, Gracie and Daisy pick their way along the fence line. The sky is lightening and the
vast horizon is beginning to appear.*}

SCENE 130 EXT. THE RABBIT-PROOF FENCE – A GRAVEL
ROAD. DAY.   {137}

*A gravel road cuts across the fence. {A gate across the road. Molly and Gracie argue while
Daisy sits watching a line of caterpillars, joined end to end like a road train, moving across
the road.}*

GRACIE: We kin go into Meeka, get the train to Wiluna.

MOLLY: They'll catch us, Gracie. {The worst bit finished. All finished. This
    way the best way.}

> *(Note: in the finished film Molly continues 'We can't stop now. We must keep going.
> We're nearly there'.)*

{GRACIE: [*scornfully*] Jigalong too far, Molly. We kin get to Wiluna easy.

MOLLY: It easy orright. Easy for them to find us. Catch us.}

GRACIE: But Molly, my mummy at Wiluna. She there.

Kenneth Branagh as Mr Neville.
Previous page: Everlyn Sampi as Molly and Tianna Sansbury as Daisy.

Tianna Sansbury as Daisy, Everlyn Sampi as Molly and Laura Monaghan as Gracie.

Everlyn Sampi as Molly.

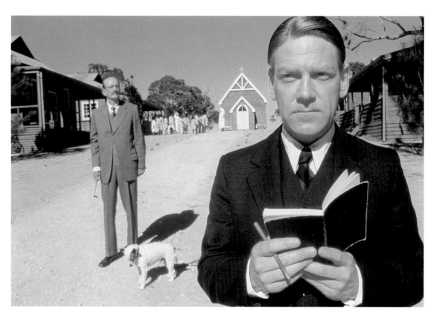

Garry McDonald as Mr Neal and Kenneth Branagh as Mr Neville.

Kenneth Branagh as Mr Neville, Everlyn Sampi as Molly and Kate Roberts as Matron.

Phillip Noyce.
Following page: Everlyn Sampi as Molly.

(Note: in the finished film Gracie says 'I want Mummy. I can't keep walking'.)
{*She sets off away from them, down the road, head down, determined. Daisy comes to stand next to Molly, grabs a piece of Molly's skirt with one hand, big eyes watching. Gracie turns, stands there, defiant.*

I'm goin' in.

Molly's shoulders slump. She gathers her bundle closer to her chest.

MOLLY: Don't go on the road, Gracie. Not on the road. Come with us around for a bit and then go in. Come with us this way.

Molly takes a few steps up the fence. Daisy lets go of her skirt, stands watching Gracie and then she begins to trudge after Molly. Molly stops, turns to plead with her.

Jes' come a little way Gracie. They get you on the road.

Daisy looks at Gracie. Gracie looks along the empty gravel road. Looks at them.}
Molly begins to walk up the fence. Daisy follows her. Gracie stands watching them. Molly walks on, Daisy following. Gracie turns, begins to walk along the road away from them.

(Note: in the finished film Molly keeps on walking and tells Daisy to 'Come on'. Daisy walks up to Gracie, and tries to pull her after Molly, then lets go and walks up to Molly, telling her 'You have to carry me'. She climbs onto Molly's back, telling her 'She not coming'. Molly tells her not to look back, that Gracie will follow. In the Scene 138, Molly lifts Daisy so she can reach into a birds nest, where there are three eggs. Molly tells Daisy 'One for you, one for me and one for both of us', and they sit and eat the eggs.)

SCENE 131 EXT. RIGGS'S CAMP – LOW HILL COUNTRY. DAY.

{134*}

Moodoo sits on the ground. He's fiddling with a twig. Behind him the fence runs off into the distance, half hidden by the low hills. Every now and then he glances south, down it.

Riggs returns from having a pee. His jacket is undone, grubby singlet underneath, wet under the armpits. Stands looking out over the white shimmering surface of the dried lake, hands on hips. His face is grimy, the sweat gleaming on his brow. He nods his head towards the desert.

RIGGS: You wouldn't catch me out there.

{*He retreats under the fly he's put up between two bushes.*}

SCENE 132 EXT. THE RABBIT-PROOF FENCE – FLAT COUNTRY.
NIGHT.   {139}

[Molly is shaking Daisy awake, gathering up her bundle. She starts walking back down the fence. Daisy runs to catch her, tugs at her skirt.

DAISY: This the wrong way, Molly. We goin' the wrong way.

Molly ignores her, pushes on. Daisy drops her things, stands there, about to cry. Molly turns, comes back to her, lets her things drop, holds Daisy by the wrists and looks directly into her eyes.]

MOLLY: We gunna go 'n find her, Dais.

They start walking back.

{SCENE 133 EXT. A COUNTRY TOWN – THE OUTSKIRTS.
MORNING.

Molly and Daisy crouch behind a bush. In the distance are the backs of a few wooden houses and the pub. Only a dog is awake, and a few town goats.

DAISY: *[whispering]* Maybe she already gone.

MOLLY: *[whispering]* Might be.

Molly scans the back yards.

DAISY: *[whispering]* Maybe that p'liceman already got her.

MOLLY: We gunna look for the train station, Daisy. You gotta keep close to me.

She sets off, running around the outskirts, keeping a good distance from the houses, Daisy shadowing her.

A young dog in a back yard sees them, stands, ears pointed, then runs, barking, along the fence. Somewhere a car door slams.

They keep running.]

SCENE 134 EXT. THE COUNTRY TOWN – THE RAILWAY
PLATFORM. MORNING.   {140}

They reach the railway line and Molly turns and runs beside it, dodging from shelter to shelter. Now they are nearing the town and she slows, finally dropping onto her stomach and pulling Daisy down beside her. Ahead of them, on the other side of the track, is a small platform. Huddled at the far end is Gracie. Daisy is exultant.

DAISY: She there, Molly, she there.

> *Molly lets out a low whistle and Gracie's head jerks up. Molly whistles again and Daisy jumps up. She signs to Gracie, a twist of the hand, 'We here. Come'. Molly pulls Daisy down sharply, her cry muffled by Molly's arm pressing her to the ground. Gracie stands, begins to gather her bundle.*

> *As Molly watches, a car edges slowly into sight from the town and begins to make its way towards the railway station.*

> *Gracie has not heard it. She is gathering her things. Molly whistles out a warning. Gracie's head jerks up. Now she hears the car. Now she sees it. She stands, frozen on the platform, now looking frantically out towards Molly, now back towards the ever approaching car. Molly whistles out again and it breaks through to Gracie. She begins to run along the platform towards them. But the car has begun to speed up and it swings into the station yard, racing along the side of the platform and coming to a halt between Gracie and the end of the platform. The door swings open and a policeman, Sergeant Mills, gets out.*

> *A bicycle wheels into the station area.*

> *Dan Willocks flings his bike down and runs to join the policeman. Gracie looks towards Molly, looks at Sergeant Mills. She gives a despairing cry but Mills already has her. (Note: in the finished film it is Dan who catches her. Gracie cries 'I want to get the train. I want to get the train to Mummy!'.) Daisy lies clinging onto Molly. They watch as Sergeant Mills talks to Gracie, the blue sleeved arm gripping the thin brown one. Dan Willocks edges in closer. Mills talks to him. Both men turn to look out beyond the track, stand there, trained eyes searching. Molly lies frozen, only her eyes watching the two men. Daisy whimpers quietly beside her.*

> *Then Gracie acts. She brings up her arm, bites the hand holding it, kicks the shins. Mills lets out a bellow, shakes his arm free. Gracie moves but Dan Willocks is quicker. He makes a grab for Gracie, gets the coat. Gracie slides out of it but Dan has a long reach. He catches her dress, then her shoulder, drops the coat to grasp her with both hands. He and Mills, now recovered, pick her up. Between them they carry her struggling to the car and bundle her roughly into the back of it. The door slams. Mills hops briskly into the driver's seat. Dan Willocks keeps guard on the back door. Molly can see Gracie's head as Gracie sits up. She sees Gracie turn to look at Dan. He is watching her. Gracie looks at Dan for a long time and then she turns her head slowly and deliberately to look to the front as the car drives off.*

(Note: in the finished film Mills tells Dan 'I'll have a shilling for you back at the station,' and then says to Gracie 'We'll take you back where you belong'.) Dan Willocks mounts his bike, follows the car.

Molly lies prone on the ground, Daisy sobbing into her neck. (Note: in the finished film Daisy says 'She gone, Molly. She not coming back'.)

The car drives out of the station and along the road back into the town, Dan pedalling along behind it.

Molly raises her head to the sky and wails soundlessly, **{***her fists tearing at her hair.***}**

{SCENE 135 INT. NEVILLE'S OFFICE. EVENING.

An empty office. Only Neville remains at work. He is deep in thought, gazing at a little figurine on his desk. It is a man carrying a kangaroo over one shoulder and two boomerangs in the other hand.

The telephone rings in Miss Thomas's office. He gets up, walks through to her room to answer it. We see him from his office, standing at her desk, his back to us.

NEVILLE: You have? Good. And her condition? Good. Very good.

Listens.

Yes, I'll make those arrangements.

Listens.

Yes. She's to go back to Moore River. And the other two? … I see. Thank you, Constable.

*Puts the phone down. Stands thinking. Walks back through to his office.***}**

SCENE 136 EXT. RIGGS'S CAMP – LOW HILL COUNTRY. DAY.

{134*, 142}

Riggs and Moodoo's swags lie out under the sun. Red sand has blown over them. Riggs is sitting under the fly. He's jotting down figures with a pencil on a crumpled piece of paper. Moodoo is sitting cross legged on the ground, fiddling with a twig. Riggs looks over to Moodoo.

RIGGS: **{**They pay you overtime for this, Moodoo?

*Moodoo looks at him. Does not reply.***}** *Riggs brushes the flies off his face. Goes to stand, staring out to the horizon over the salt lake.*

{It's like a flippin'} needle in a haystack.

{*Moodoo begins to draw in the sand with the twig.*} *(Note: in the finished film Riggs, looking at the desert, says 'Well, that's it. Pack your stuff. We're getting out of here. They're only paying us for three weeks', and Moodoo smiles. The following dialogue occurs in Scene 132.)*

MOODOO: She pretty clever one, that one.

He looks up at Riggs.

She wanna get home.

{*Riggs looks over to him, seeing him for the first time.*

RIGGS: Where your country?

Moodoo jerks his head up the fence, same direction.

MOODOO: North. Kimberleys.

RIGGS: You don't want to go home?

Moodoo doesn't answer. He is drawing a map in the sand with a twig. Riggs turns, walks over to his swag. He throws the blanket down on top of it.

We could be stuck out here forever. I've bloody had it. Let's go.

Moodoo smooths the drawing over with his hand, obliterates it. He takes the 'twig' and snaps it. Throws the pieces aside. They lie on the ground.

A wooden clothes peg.}

{SCENE 137 EXT. THE DESERT. NIGHT.

Molly and Daisy sleep not far from the fence, covered by Molly's coat.}

SCENE 138 EXT. A STONE LANDSCAPE. NIGHT.   {141}

Molly and Daisy walk through an immense stone landscape. {*A flock of cockatoos swoops over them, flies away to the east.*}

{SCENE 139 EXT. A DESERT ROCK POOL. EVENING.

Molly collects water from a rock pool with her tin. Drinks. Gives some to Daisy.}

SCENE 140 INT./EXT. NEVILLE'S OFFICE. DAY.   {144}

(Note: in the finished film, Scene 143 is a montage of Molly and Daisy walking through sand hills.) {*Neville at the door of his office, the wording in gold, 'Chief Protector', framing his head.*}

NEVILLE: {Miss Thomas, when you have a moment.}

> *He goes back into his room, stands looking down at the queue of people waiting outside in the sun. A girl of about ten stands holding her mother's hand.*

> {*Miss Thomas comes in. He remains standing at the window, looking down.*}

Can you take a letter to Constable Riggs, please, Miss Thomas?}

> *He dictates, still at the window.*

'The two half-caste girls, Molly and Daisy, are returning to Jigalong via the rabbit-proof fence. All our efforts to apprehend them so far having come to nought. I expect them to arrive at Jigalong in around one month's time. In your capacity as local protector you are to proceed to Jigalong to await their arrival and effect their recapture. Yours …' et cetera.

> *He turns, looks at her.*

{It's just occurred to me: the little one is the same age as my Peter.}

{SCENE 141 EXT. SAND HILLS. MORNING.

Molly and Daisy walk, the fence nearby.}

SCENE 142 EXT. THE RABBIT-PROOF FENCE – FLAT DESERT. AFTERNOON.   {145*}

Molly and Daisy struggle through fearsome country; long, spinifex-covered sand ridges. The sand is banked up against the fence, nearly burying it. Molly leads and Daisy stumbles along behind her. Molly is carrying her coat and bag. Daisy carries only her bag.

The desert stretches remorselessly before them, malign, beautiful, overpowering. {*Through it, for as far as the eye can see, the faint track of the fence.*}

{SCENE 143 EXT. THE RABBIT-PROOF FENCE – FLAT DESERT. NIGHT.

Molly and Daisy sleep under the greatcoat. Molly twists and murmurs in her sleep. A dingo howls.}

Everlyn Sampi as Molly and Tianna Sansbury as Daisy.

{SCENE 144 EXT. THE RABBIT-PROOF FENCE – FLAT DESERT. MORNING.

Molly is shaking Daisy awake.

MOLLY: C'mon Daisy. Wake up. We gotta keep goin'.

   Daisy is weak and groggy. Flies settle around her parched lips. Molly hauls her up.

DAISY: Hungry.

MOLLY: We get somethin' soon, Daisy. C'mon.

   She takes Daisy's arm, leads her along.}

SCENE 145 EXT. THE RABBIT-PROOF FENCE – A SALT PAN. DAY.   {145*}

Molly is carrying Daisy on her back beside the fence. She walks with her head down, dogged. After a few steps she looks up.

Stops.

Lets Daisy slide from her back as she stares out across a flat, endless salt pan. She looks along the fence which continues out into the salt pan and ends. After it, nothing. The salt pan stretches out into the distance, endless. Unmarked. Only a shimmer on the horizon. (Note: in the finished film Molly sobs when the fence ends, and Daisy tells her that she wants mother. Molly continues on, saying 'That fence will come back'. Scene 146 is a montage of shots of Molly and Gracie continuing across the desert: Molly drinking water through grass; the girls continuing to walk through a heat haze; Molly carrying Daisy, until she begins to stagger and falls to the ground. Scene 147 shows Maude and Frinda in Jigalong, holding the fence and singing.)

{*Daisy looks up at Molly. Molly looks out across the expanse. She is utterly defeated. Sinks to the ground.*}

SCENE 146 EXT. {THE RABBIT-PROOF FENCE }– THE SALT PAN. DAY.   {148}

Molly and Daisy lie {near the fence, under the coat.} The sun is high in the sky. Daisy sleeps fitfully, twisting and jerking. {Molly pushes the coat off, crawls to the fence. She pulls herself up and sits propped against it. She looks north, the way ahead. The salt pan stretches out remorselessly, never ending. She looks at Daisy, at the flies gathering around her eyes and mouth. She slumps down. Crawls back to Daisy. Pulls the coat over her. Closes her eyes.}

SCENE 147 EXT. {THE RABBIT-PROOF FENCE} – THE SALT PAN. {NIGHT.   {150}

Molly and Daisy are sleeping under Molly's coat.

A moonlit night. The sound of a dingo howling.}

(Note: in the finished film Scene 149 is Maude and Frinda sitting by the fence, singing. This scene is set during the day, in the middle of the salt pan.) Molly stirs, moans in her sleep. Wakes. Her eyes flicker open. A black and brown hawk {is sitting on a fence post looking at her. Molly looks at the hawk. Does not see it. It stays there, looking directly at her. Her eyes begin to focus. The hawk rests on the post, displaying itself to her, its black eyes penetrating her. Molly sees the hawk clearly. It's strength and power. Its absolute beauty, fierce and wild.

The hawk opens its wings, stays looking at her, before lifting itself leisurely into the air,} circling and then flying off. Molly lies on the ground looking up {at the stars high in the black sky.

She begins to sing. One line, then the next, in language. Daisy turns, opens her eyes, watches her. She repeats the lines, tapping gently on the ground with her hand. Daisy raises herself on one arm.

DAISY: You got new song, Molly?}

> *(Note: in the finished film Molly watches the hawk, then picks up Daisy and continues on her walk home.)*

{SCENE 148 EXT. THE EDGE OF THE SALT PAN. MORNING.

Molly is standing looking out across the salt pan. Her coat and bag discarded. Daisy comes to stand beside her, grabs a piece of her skirt. Molly looks down at her.

MOLLY: You think those legs gunna make it?

> *Daisy looks down at her legs, the open, weeping sores. She holds one leg out, tries to see the back of it.*

They reach the ground don't they?

> *Daisy looks at her. Nods. Molly shrugs.*

That all right, then. Come on.

She takes a deep breath. Sets her sights to the shimmering horizon. Begins to walk along the fence towards the pan. Daisy follows.}

{SCENE 149 EXT. THE SALT PAN. DAY.

Molly and Daisy walk in the middle of the pan. Molly stops. Looks around.

Molly's point of view: on all sides, and for as far as she can see, the brown, parched earth. Now, just as when they were taken at the Depot and in the cabin at sea, the world turns as she looks around. There is no sound. No life. Earth and sky merge into one.

She stands absolutely still.

Daisy puts out her hand to touch her.

The world stops turning.

Molly starts walking again.}

SCENE 150 EXT. MONTAGE. DAY.   {146}

Crossing the salt pan.

The girls walking. Shimmering haze. Shadows. Sun. {Footprints stretching out behind them. Digging hands reaching to the bottom of a hole to scoop out a handful of dirty water. Aerial shots. Camera looking directly down on them.} Molly carrying Daisy.

{SCENE 151 EXT. THE SALT PAN. DAY.

Molly is struggling across the salt pan, Daisy following behind her.

Far ahead, out of the shimmer, comes a darker ridge. Molly sees it. Quickens her pace. Walks on, her head slightly raised as if to smell the air for desert plants.

And then it appears out of the haze: the fence. Continuing on, out of the salt pan and beyond. In the far distance the faint shimmer of the Jigalong hills.

Molly stops. Breathes in the sight. Turns to Daisy.

MOLLY: Now we right.}

SCENE 152 EXT. THE RABBIT-PROOF FENCE – JIGALONG. DAY. {151}

Riggs's car driving along a road through the desert towards Jigalong. In the near distance those distinctive hills of Jigalong.

SCENE 153 INT. NEVILLE'S OFFICE. AFTERNOON. {152}

Neville at his desk. The door is open through to Miss Thomas. She is sitting at her desk, one ear to the telephone. She calls through to him.

MISS THOMAS: It's coming through now.

> *He sits. She relays the message to him.*

Riggs arrived Jigalong. Awaits your instructions. [*Into the phone*] Yes, there will be a reply. Can you hold the line please?

SCENE 154 EXT. A SHED – JIGALONG DEPOT. AFTERNOON. {153}

Hungerford sits at a small table outside, listening through a set of headphones. He writes down the message. He looks over to Riggs who is sitting, smoking. He reads.

HUNGERFORD: Girls to be sent south via Meekatharra. To be accompanied at all times. Awaiting notification.

> *Riggs grunts. Taps the ash off his cigarette. In the distance the sounds of women singing. Riggs nods in their direction.*

RIGGS: What's that all about?

HUNGERFORD: Some women's business. It's been going on all week. {Be over soon.}

SCENE 155 EXT. SCRUB – JIGALONG. DUSK. {154}

Molly and Daisy creep through the bush, the sounds drifting towards them. (Note: in the finished film Daisy asks 'That tracker, he not going to get us now?'. Molly replies 'No, he not going to get us'.) {And then a hand reaches out, grabs Molly. Pulls her up. Molly looks into the face of a woman, the lookout.

LOOKOUT: [*in language*] Come with me.}

{SCENE 156 EXT. THE SHED – JIGALONG DEPOT. DUSK.

Riggs sits with Hungerford.

RIGGS: I don't like it. There's something not right.

HUNGERFORD: It happens around this time every year.

RIGGS: Gives me the creeps.

He shivers, reaches around for his jacket, cigarette in mouth.}

{SCENE 157 EXT. SCRUB – JIGALONG. DUSK.

Molly and Daisy are led through the scrub, the sounds coming in and out of the night to them. They can see now the flickering fires.}

SCENE 158 EXT. THE SHED – JIGALONG DEPOT. DUSK. {155}

Riggs and Hungerford.

RIGGS: I'm not going to just sit here. I can feel it.

He flicks his cigarette butt out into the night.

They're up to something. I'm going to take a look.

{Hungerford is disturbed.

HUNGERFORD: You can't go now, man. It's dark. And you certainly can't go onto the women's ground.

Riggs stands, tightens his belt and reaches for the rifle leaning against the wall.

RIGGS: I can go wherever I like.}

SCENE 159 EXT. THE WOMEN'S PLACE – THE SCRUB. NIGHT.

{156}

Frinda is singing. A group of women, painted with black dust and red ochre, are dancing. They shuffle forward, feet scuffing through the soft earth, deep in the rhythm. Low fires flicker.

SCENE 160 EXT. THE CAMP – JIGALONG. NIGHT.   {157}

Riggs walks through the camp to the women's ground. The men sit at their fires watching silently as he stumbles around the trees. The song comes to him out of the night, drawing him onwards.

Jason Clarke as Riggs.

{SCENE 161 EXT. THE SCRUB – JIGALONG. NIGHT.

The lookout leads Molly and Daisy on towards the song and the fires.}

SCENE 162 EXT. THE WOMEN'S PLACE – THE SCRUB. NIGHT.

{158*}

{*The song ends and the women shrug their shoulders, hold their arms out. Take a few steps back.*} *They can hear Riggs stumbling through the bush. They listen as he stumbles towards them through the dark.* {*Frinda stands, dusts off her hands. She takes a blanket to cover the designs on her body and steps forward, away from the group, to meet him. Maude covers herself and joins her.*}

{SCENE 163 EXT. HIGH GROUND – JIGALONG. NIGHT.

The lookout leads Molly and Daisy towards the fires.}

SCENE 164 EXT. THE WOMEN'S PLACE – THE SCRUB. NIGHT.

{158*}

Frinda and Maude, blankets around them, stand waiting. Riggs appears out of the night. He is breathing heavily, his jacket unbuttoned. He holds the rifle down at his side. Frinda takes a step towards him, stands there in the night. Tiny but powerful.

{FRINDA: This woman's place, p'liceman. You better go.}

> *Riggs peers into the dark beyond her, can see dim bodies in the firelight. He looks at Frinda, looks at Maude at her side. Maude stands quiet, watchful.*

{You better go, p'liceman. You better go or we sing you love magic, maybe.

> *She laughs a deep-throated laugh. Maude laughs. The women around all laugh.*}
> *Riggs looks startled. Looks all around.* {*Looks at the black women's faces laughing at him. Someone says something in language and all the women laugh once more.*}
> *Riggs takes a step back. And then another. Then he turns and walks away, back to the Depot.*

SCENE 165 EXT. HIGH GROUND – JIGALONG. NIGHT. {158*}

Molly is walking slowly with Daisy, eyes straining out into the night. Two shapes are coming towards her through the dark. She stops, stands, eyes peering out into the blackness. Daisy stands close by her, clinging on to her arm. Molly can hardly breathe. One of the figures, the bigger one, stops, draws her blanket around her shoulders. And then the tiny one comes to stand beside her. Molly takes a step out, towards the flickering fires. Daisy steps out too. Then Molly runs. And calls. Dodging through the bushes, skirting the trees. Now she can see that it is Maude and Maude is calling to her, arms outstretched. Molly runs towards Maude's arms. And Maude's brown arms, arms painted with the red and white and black designs, reach out for her, pull her into them. Maude holds her daughter to her. Begins to wail, rocking Molly deep in her arms.

SCENE 166 EXT. HIGH GROUND – JIGALONG. NIGHT. {158*}

Molly stands before Frinda, head downcast. She can't look at her.

MOLLY: I lost one. I lost one.

> *Frinda wraps her scrawny arms around Molly. Pulls her toward her. Beside her Maude cradles Daisy. And then Frinda wails. She wails for the granddaughter who has come back and for the granddaughter she has lost. The two rock together, Molly resting in her arms, the black head against the old grey one.*

{SCENE 167 EXT. THE WOMEN'S PLACE – THE SCRUB. NIGHT.

Molly kneels on the ground, her head held proud. Daisy watches. Maude bends, singing, as she marks Molly's chest. Frinda sings as her fingers paint red ochre on Molly's shoulders. The song washes over Molly and goes out into the night.}

{SCENE 168 EXT. JIGALONG DEPOT. MORNING.

The first traces of light on the vast horizon. The Depot and the rabbit-proof fence. Riggs's car sitting, waiting.

Silence.}

SCENE 169 EXT. THE CAMP – JIGALONG. DAY.   {160}

{*In the riverbed, the shapes of the bower shelters. A few shadows are moving out from the camp.*} *A small band makes its way. We can see the shapes of Molly and Daisy, Frinda with a stick, Maude. They are walking away from the camp. Into the desert.*

(Note: in the finished film Molly speaks in dialect, in a voice over. 'We walked for nine weeks, a long way, all the way home. Then we went straightaway and hid in the desert.' Scene 161 is a montage the desert and mottled plains. Molly continues her voice over. 'Got married. I had two baby girls. Then they took me and my kids back to that place, Moore River. And I walked all the way back to Jigalong again, carrying Annabella, the little one. When she was three, that Mr Neville took her away. I've never seen her again. Gracie is dead now. She never made it back to Jigalong. Daisy and me, we're here, living in our country, Jigalong. We're never going back to that place.')

SCENE 170 INT./EXT. NEVILLE'S OFFICE. DAY.   {159, 162*}

We are looking out the window of Neville's office. A queue of Aborigines stand in the sun. They chat and laugh among themselves.

Neville stands looking down at them. He is dictating a letter to Miss Thomas who sits at his desk. At some point in the letter he returns to sit.

NEVILLE: '{Thank you for your report dated the fourteenth inst. regarding the missing half-caste girls, Molly and Daisy.} I would ask to be kept informed of their whereabouts so that at some future date they can be recovered. We have an uphill battle with these people, especially the bush natives, who have to be protected against themselves. If they would only understand what we are trying to do for them. Yours …' et cetera.

> *Miss Thomas leaves. He takes a card from one of the neat piles covering his desk and begins to write. As he continues these titles roll up:*
>
> *'Mr Neville was Chief Protector of Aborigines in Western Australia for 25 years. He retired in 1940.*
>
> *'Australian Aboriginal children continued to be removed from their families under government policy until 1970.' (Note: in the finished film another card reads 'Today many of these Aboriginal people continue to suffer from this destruction of identity, family life and culture. We call them the Stolen Generations.' These titles fade in and out over black before the end credits.)*

SCENE 171 EXT. JIGALONG. DAY.   {162*}

Dissolve to the present day.

The real Molly, 84, and Daisy, 78, are standing in the riverbed at Jigalong.

Titles continue:

{ *'Molly married and had two children.*

'She, and her children aged 4 and 2, were all taken back to Moore River Native Settlement.

'Molly walked back to Jigalong again, carrying Annabelle, the baby, and leaving Doris, the eldest, at Moore River.

'When Annabelle was 3 she was taken from Molly. Molly has never seen her again.

'Doris was reunited with her mother 30 years later. She wrote her mother's story on which this film is based.

'Gracie was taken back to Moore River. As a young girl she worked as a servant. She died in 1983. She never made it back to Jigalong.

'Molly and Daisy are still living in Jigalong today. }

Molly stands proud and erect, her chin high, looking straight to camera. Daisy is talking to Molly. They laugh.

Fade out.

Everlyn Sampi as Molly and Ningali Lawford as Maude.

Film End Credits

Based on the book by Molly's daughter DORIS PILKINGTON GARIMARA / Molly EVERLYN SAMPI / Daisy TIANNA SANSBURY / Gracie LAURA MONAGHAN / Moodoo DAVID GULPILIL / Molly's Mother NINGALI LAWFORD / Molly's Grandmother MYARN LAWFORD / Mavis DEBORAH MAILMAN / Constable Riggs JASON CLARKE / Mr Neville KENNETH BRANAGH.

Directed by PHILLIP NOYCE / Screenplay by CHRISTINE OLSEN / Produced by PHILLIP NOYCE, CHRISTINE OLSEN / Producer JOHN WINTER / Executive Producers DAVID ELFICK, JEREMY THOMAS, KATHLEEN McLAUGHLIN / Children's Drama Coach RACHAEL MAZA / Director Of Photography CHRISTOPHER DOYLE H.K.S.C / Production Designer & Costume Designer ROGER FORD / Edited by JOHN SCOTT, VERONIKA JENET / Music by PETER GABRIEL / Music Arranged & Mixed by RICHARD EVANS, DAVID RHODES / Sound Designer CRAIG CARTER / Supervising Sound Editor JOHN PENDERS / Music Supervisor GEORGE ACOGNY / Casting CHRISTINE KING / 2nd Unit Director IAN JONES / 1st Assistant Director EMMA SCHOFIELD / Associate Producer LAURA BURROWS

Dormitory Boss (Nina) NATASHA WANGANEEN / Mr Neal GARRY MCDONALD / Police Inspector ROY BILLING / Miss Thomas LORNA LESLIE / Miss Jessop CELINE O'LEARY / Matron KATE ROBERTS / Moodoo's Daughter TRACY MONAGHAN / Escaped Girl (Olive) TAMARA FLANAGAN / Kangaroo Hunter DAVID NGOOMBUJARRA / the Fence Builder ANTHONY HAYES / Depot Manager ANDREW S GILBERT / Gracie's Mother SHERYL CARTER / Wiluna Liar HEATH BERGERSON / Moore River Policeman TREVOR JAMIESON / First Farm Mother

EDWINA BISHOP / Farm Daughter KERILEE MEURIS / Car Driving Policeman ANDREW MARTIN / Fence Worker KEN RADLEY / Mr Evans DON BARKER / Mrs Evans CARMEL JOHNSON / Policeman At Railway DAVID BUCHANAN / Policeman At Evans' Farmhouse RICHARD CARTER / Jigalong Mother FIONA GREGORY / Tommy Grant REGGIE WANGANEEN / Woman In Queue GLENYS SAMPI / First Dormitory Girl KIZZY FLANAGAN / Second Dormitory Girl ANTONIA SAMPI / Aboriginal Hunter MAURICE KELLY / Jigalong Extras JANGANPA GROUP / Singing Women At Jigalong ELSIE THOMAS, ROSIE GOODJI, JEWESS JAMES, JANGANPA GROUP / Molly Doubles CONNIE AMOS, RAQUEL KERDEL, AMELIA DANN / Gracie Doubles VERNA LAWRIE, ERIN WILSON / Daisy Doubles CERRIN KARPANY, DANNI-RAE WILSON.

Co-Executive Producers JONATHAN SHTEINMAN, EMILE SHERMAN / Production Manager JULIE SIMS / Script Supervisor KRISTIN WITCOMBE / Script Editor ALISON TILSON / 2nd Assistant Director DEBORAH ANTONIOU / 3rd Assistant Directors JULIE WILSON, EDDIE THORNE / 4th Assistant Director DUAN KERERU / Production Co-ordinator SUZANNE MALLOS / Travel Co-ordinator LINDY TAYLOR / Assistant Travel Co-ordinator SUE BENNETT / Production Secretary JESSICA BRENTNALL / Production Runner CHRIS TAYLOR / Additional Photography BRAD SHIELD / Focus Puller KATRINA CROOK / Clapper Loader SIMON WILLIAMS / Additional Clapper Loader LUCINDA VAN DE BERKT / Video Split Operator JIMMY SMITH

Gaffer NICK PAYNE / Best Boy GLEN JENKINS / 3rd Electrics LIAM ADAM / Key Grip ROBIN MORGAN / Grip JIM McINTOSH / Additional Grips ANDY SMITH, RICK BELFIELD / Production Sound Recordist BRONWYN A. MURPHY / Boom Operator STEPHEN JACKSON-VAUGHAN / 2nd Unit Director Of Photography, Steadicam Operator & Aerial Photography IAN JONES / 2nd Unit Focus Puller PETER WHITE / 2nd Unit Assistant Director ROSS FARGHER / 2nd Unit Continuity LUCIA NOYCE / Art Director LAURIE FAEN / Assistant Art Director BEN MORIESON / Art Department Co-ordinator JOCELYN THOMAS / Set Decorator REBECCA COHEN / Assistant Set Decorator ANNE HARRY / Props Buyer ROBERT WEBB / Standby Props DEAN SULLIVAN / Art Department Assistant & Armourer SONNY PILKINGTON / Art Department Runner ROBERT CROMPTON / Standby Painter KYLIE LAWSON / Vehicle Co-ordinator & Rain Effects JONATHAN BLAIKIE / Construction

Manager JOHN MOORE / Leading Hand MICHAEL THOMAS / Set Construction RON PRIOR, JEFF PRIOR / Carpenters MATTHEW HARRY, BEN NAUGHTON, DAVID O'REILLY, PAUL O'REILLY / Trades Assistants SHANE BADCOE, STEVE CRAIG, CHRIS LANDRETH, MATTHEW LANDRETH, JOHN WIGHT / Labourers ANTHONY MEZIC, ANDREW MILLER, JUSTIN NAUGHTON, PAUL NAUGHTON, ALUN SYMES / Fence Construction IAN FERGUSON, CORKY RESCHKE / Scenic Artist GUY ALLAIN / Set Finisher GINA ALLAIN / Painter MANDY CHAPMAN / Brush Hands LAILA ALLAIN, DAVID GOLDSWORTHY, LUKE JOHNSTON, JENNY WOODLEY / Assistant Costume Designer & Costume Supervisor RUTH DE LA LANDE / Costume Standby JULIE KRUGER / Assistant Standby ZEYNEP SELCUK / Costumier JUDITH MATTERS / Seamstress PAT BLACKSTOCK / Hair & Make-Up Supervisor KATE BIRCH / Hair & Make-Up Artist SIMONE WAJON / Horse Wrangler BILL WILLOUGHBY / Dog Wrangler SINDY & ALICIA MCCOURT / Camel Wrangler DON AZIZ / Goanna Wrangler GAVIN FOREMAN – SCALES & TAILS / Hawk Wrangler ANDREW PAYNE / Prosthetic Goanna ROBINSON'S THEMESCAPES

Location Manager – Flinders Ranges MAUDE HEATH / Location Manager – Adelaide MARK EVANS / Location Assistant – Adelaide RITA ZANCHETTA / Unit Manager WIL MILNE / On-Set Unit Manager KIM GLADMAN / Unit Assistants ANDREW HAYES, OWEN LOVE / Night Unit Assistant GRAEME DUFFEY / Stunt Coordinator EDDY MCSHORTALL / Assistant Safety Supervisor RUSSELL ALLAN / Precision Driver MARK CAMPBELL / Casting Assistant CHRISTINA NO / Casting Associates BROOKE HOWDEN, JODIE MCKENNA / Western Australian Casting ANNIE MURTAGH-MONKS, JENNI COHEN, RIC BRAYFORD / Northern Territory Casting MAGGIE MILES / Alice Springs Casting LIZ HUGHES / Extras Casting – Leigh Creek COLIN MURDOCH, HEATHER COLMAN / Extras Casting – Adelaide ANGELA HESSOM, JULIA LEWINGTON / Extras Casting – Alice Springs VAST FILM & PHOTOGRAPHY, PETER YATES / Assistant to Phillip Noyce MIRANDA CULLEY / Assistant to David Elfick JOCELYN QUIOC / Assistant to Kathleen Mclaughlin CORY MCCALL / Attachments to Phillip Noyce DARLENE JOHNSON, DANIELLE MACLEAN / Extras Driver/Rushes Runner GEOFFREY HALLORAN / Cast Driver MIKE McDERMOTT / Double Drivers NOEL WILTON, JADE BRADY, KIM NESTOR / Publicity EMMA COOPER / Stills Photographers MERVYN BISHOP, PENNY

TWEEDIE, MATTHEW NETTHEIM, LISA TOMASETTI, GRAHAM SHEARER / Accounting Services MONEYPENNY SERVICES / Production Accountant JANE SMITH / Assistant Accountant JENNY HAGLEY / Post Production Accountant DENISE FARRELL, JILL COVERDALE / Catering – Adelaide EVANGELINE FEARY – FOOD NOIR / Catering – Flinders Ranges STEVE MARCUS FILM CATERING, PHIL PIKE / Script Consultant DORIS PILKINGTON GARIMARA / Wangajunka Language Consultant NINGALI LAWFORD / Tutor MONICA SWAN / Doubles Minder KIMBERLEY NESTOR / Singing Teacher ROSALIND AYLMORE / Unit Nurse JACQUIE ROBERTSON / Jigalong Community Advisor BRIAN SAMSON

Additional Crew 1st Assistant Directors KAREN MAHOOD, VICKI SUGARS, CHRIS LYNCH / 2nd Assistant Director IAN HAMILTON / 3rd Assistant Director SARAH SPILLANE / Focus Puller LUKE NIXON / Clapper Loader LEE MARIANO / Camera Assistant KEVIN SCOTT / Sound Recordist BEN OSMO / Boom Operator GERRY NUCIFORA / Gaffer MILES JONES / Best Boy ADAM HUNTER / Electrics ANGUS KEMP / NATHAN WALTON / Key Grip DAVE NICHOLS / Grips SIMON BONNEY, ROB WILKINS / Assistant Grips JAMES HOPWOOD, STUART BELL / Luggers RORY RISKY, KEN THOMAS / Art Director BEN MORIESON / Art Department Assistant ALICE LODGE / Fencing Contractors GIDDIUP FENCING / Special Effects PRIDE EFFECTS / Additional Hair & Makeup Artist TERRI FARMER / Costumes SUE MILES, AMANDA IRVING, MEL DYKES / Production Co-ordinators REBECCA SUMMERTON, HEATHER MUIRHEAD / Production Assistant MELISSA HASLUCK / Cast Liaison MICHELLE ADAMS / Production Runner PETER WISEMAN / Safety Officers GORDAN WADDELL, LOU CIFUENTES / Catering CAMERA COOKS, CLAIRE POLLARD / Post Production Supervisor HELEN PANCKHURST / 1st Assistant Editors BRIDGETTE FAHEY-GOLDSMITH, LISA-ANNE MORRIS / 2nd Assistant Editors ANTONIO MESTRES, ALLISON GIBBONS / Sound Post Production Facility SOUNDFIRM AUSTRALIA / ADR Recording BLAIR SLATER / MICHAEL THOMPSON, ANDREW WRIGHT / ADR Editors RICKY EDWARDS, ANDREW PLAIN / Foley Recordist & Mixer STEVE BURGESS / Foley Artist GERARD LONG / Re-Recording Mixers IAN MCLOUGHLIN C.A..S., ROGER SAVAGE / Dolby Sound Consultant STEVE MURPHY / Visual Effects by ANIMAL LOGIC FILM / Visual Effects Supervisor MURRAY POPE / Visual Effects Producer FIONA

CRAWFORD / Visual Effects Coordinator BEN CAINE / Supervising Compositor KIRSTY MILLAR / Senior Compositor KRISTA JORDAN / Compositors MARK BARBER, DAVE DALLEY, JEAN-MARC FURIO / Assistant Compositor IVAN MORAN / Matte Painter GRANT FRECKLETON / Film Bureau Supervisor CHRIS SWINBANKS / Scanning and Recording Operators MARK HARMON, JOHN POPE / Visual Effects by FUEL INTERNATIONAL / Visual Effects Supervisor PAUL BUTTERWORTH / Senior Compositor DAVE MORLEY / 3D Technical Director SIMON MADDISON / Visual Effects Producer JASON BATH / Visual Effects by GMD / Executive Producer PETER FISHER / Visual Effects Producer DAVID HEWITT / Senior Compositor ANDREW MCKENNA / Compositor CHRIS LEAVER, HUGH SEVILLE / IT Wrangler CLAYTON BELL / Technical Director PETER KING / Editing Facilities ISLAND FILMS, SPECTRUM FILMS / Film Laboratory ATLAB AUSTRALIA / Laboratory Liaison IAN RUSSELL / Digital Opticals ANTHOS SIMON, ROBERT SANDEMAN, HENRY YEKANIANS / Colour Grader ARTHUR CAMBRIDGE / Director of Productions, Atlab OLIVIER FONTENAY / Neg Matching NEGATIVE CUTTING SERVICES (AUST) PTY LTD / Telecine Transfer VIDEO 8 BROADCAST / Title Design OLIVER STREETON, PETER NEWTON / Title Production AMANDA NEWTON, OPTICAL & GRAPHIC

Fujifilm Stocks FILM SUPPORT / Kodak Film Stock KODAK AUSTRALASIA / Two Way Radios MULTICOM COMMUNICATIONS / Freight Services AUSFILM TRANSPORT & LOGISTICS, GABRIELLE MCKECHNIE / Travel & Vehicles SHOWFILM / Make-Up Van IRONBARK HOLDINGS / Costume Van EMPIRE PRODUCTION SERVICES / Helicopter Mounts CONTINENTAL MOUNTS AUSTRALIA / Helicopter Charter HELICOPTERS AUSTRALIA / Helicopter Pilot BRIAN HOLE / Production Lawyers STEVENSON COURT LAWYERS, NINA STEVENSON / Insurance Broker HW WOOD AUSTRALIA PTY LTD, TONY GIBBS / Completion Guarantor FILM FINANCES, INC / Auditors CHRISTOPHER COOTE & CO. / World Revenues Collected & Distributed by FINTAGE COLLECTION ACCOUNT MANAGEMENT BV / Additional Research LINLEY BATTERHAM / Library Footage Supplied by FILM AUSTRALIA LIBRARY / Steam Train Footage from "A STEAM TRAIN PASSES" / Director: David Haythornthwaite / Producer: Anthony Buckley / Perth Period Footage From "SUNNY SOUTH WEST" DEPARTMENT OF COMMERCE / Australian Music Supervisor

CHRISTINE WOODRUFF / Music Editors JOE E. RAND, JULIE PEARCE / Music Recorded at REAL WORLD / Music Produced by RICHARD EVANS, PETER GABRIEL, DAVID RHODES / Assisted by EDEL GRIFFITH / Additional Engineering RICHARD CHAPPELL / Music for the end title theme

"NGANKARRPARNI" (Sky Blue Reprise) by Peter Gabriel, Featuring the Blind Boys of Alabama and Myarn and Ningali Lawford

"THE MASKED MASQUERADERS" Episode 5, Courtesy of 4BC Brisbane

"THE MAN WHO BROKE THE BANK AT MONTE CARLO" Written by Fred Gilbert, Recording courtesy of De Wolfe Music

Photograph's Courtesy of WESTERN AUSTRALIAN NEWSPAPERS LIMITED, BRENDT MUSEUM OF ANTHROPOLOGY, UNIVERSITY OF WESTERN AUSTRALIA, THE BATTYE LIBRARY PICTORIAL COLLECTION, THE MOGUMBAR HERITAGE COMMITTEE PICTORIAL COLLECTION

Producers wish to thank The Jigalong Community, The Kuyani and the Adnyahmathna people, the traditional owners of the land, for their permission to film in the Flinders Ranges. The Kaurna Meyunna Association and the Mannum Aboriginal Consultative Committee Guarna Peramangk. Mogumber Heritage Committee, Beverley & Stuart Patterson, Claire Dobbin, Bill Ross, Bob and Myrna Tonkinson, Dr John Von Sturmer, The Port Dock Railway Museum, Urrbrae House, Tineriba Tribal Gallery, The Banana Room, Year 5 Darlington Public School 2001, Onkaparinga National Park, Department for Environment & Heritage, South Australia. Belair National Park, Terry Gregory - District Ranger, Richard Coombe - Sturt District Senior Ranger, South Australian Police Department, Chirsties Beach Traffic Department, Dr Rosemary Brooks, St Ann's College - North Adelaide, State Library Of South Australia, Sharp Direct, James Thomas, Paul Castley, McAlpine House Broome, Mambo, General Pants, Bonds, Cody Premium Outdoor. The People Of Leigh Creek, Flinders Ranges and Parachilna

DIGITAL DTS SOUND (LOGO) / SDDS (LOGO) / DOLBY DIGITAL (LOGO) IN SELECTED THEATRES / CAMERA AND LENSES SUPPLIED BY PANAVISION AUSTRALIA PTY LTD

Doris Pilkington Garimara's book 'Follow The Rabbit-Proof Fence' is Published by UNIVERSITY OF QUEENSLAND PRESS

The painting songs sung by The Walpiri, Amatjere and Wangajunka Women were not sacred songs but were songs able to be performed in public.

International Distribution by (HANWAY LOGO)

Developed in association with the AUSTRALIAN FILM COMMISSION (AFC LOGO)

Developed with the assistance of SCREENWEST and THE LOTTERIES COMMISSION OF WESTERN AUSTRALIA

Produced with the assistance of and finance from the SOUTH AUSTRALIAN FILM CORPORATION In association with THE PREMIUM MOVIE PARTNERSHIP FOR SHOWTIME AUSTRALIA

Financed with the assistance of (FFC LOGO)

No animals were harmed in the making of this film.

Filmed on location in Adelaide and the Flinders Ranges of South Australia and the Pilbara region of Western Australia

Copyright in this cinematogrpahic film (including, without limitation, the soundtrack thereof) is protected under the laws of Australia and other countries. Unauthorised copying, duplication or exhibition may result in civil liability and criminal prosecution.

© 2002 Australian Film Finance Corporation Limited, The Premium Movie Partnership, South Australian Film Corporation and Jabal Films Pty Ltd.

Other Screenplays from Currency Press

Andrew Bovell
LANTANA
A woman disappears, and four marriages are drawn into a tangled web of love, deceit, sex and death. Not all of them will survive. *Lantana* is an intriguing drama about love, infidelity, mistrust and mistakes. Based on the internationally-produced play by Andrew Bovell, *Speaking in Tongues.*

'A literate, densely layered, seamlessly constructed script ... a moody, intensely emotional thriller...' Erin Free, *If Magazine*
0 86819 659 2

Andrew Dominik
CHOPPER
This provocative screenplay takes us inside the mind of Mark Brandon 'Chopper' Read, one of Australia's most notorious criminals, whose sometimes violent antics have earned him cult status. Includes an introduction from the writer-director, a foreword by Mark Read and stills from the film.

'It's a terrific script—wildly entertaining, well-written and surprisingly touching.' Annie Nocenti, Editor, *Scenario,* New York
0 86819 642 8

Shirley Barrett
LOVE SERENADE
Sisters Dimity and Vicki-Ann live in a forlorn Riverina town. Enter Ken Sherry, the ex-drive-time king of Brisbane radio who takes over the running of the local radio station. Exit sibling loyalty as the sisters battle for his affections.
0 86819 529 4

Robert Caswell
SCALES OF JUSTICE
A subtle and scrupulous examination of how and why organised crime flourishes in Australia. This series drew acclaim and outraged protests in equal measure when first screened on the ABC. Winner of a TV AWGIE award.
0 86819 097 7

Paul Cox
3 SCREENPLAYS
Co-written with John Clarke, Bob Ellis and Barry Dickins respectively, these screenplays make a trilogy of love and death. *Lonely Hearts* is a story of first love; *My First Wife* is the story of the disintegration of a relationship; and *A Woman's Tale* is about a woman succumbing to cancer.
0 86819 547 2

Rolf de Heer
BAD BOY BUBBY
A powerful and disturbing 'de profundis' story. Bubby escapes from the subterranean depths of a brutalising and hermetic childhood, into a world that seems more damaged than the hellhole from which he has emerged.
0 86819 426 3

Stephan Elliott
THE ADVENTURES OF PRISCILLA, QUEEN OF THE DESERT
This award-winning film follows three showgirls-with-a-difference on their hilarious and outrageous journey through the outback of Australia in a bus called Priscilla.
0 86819 416 6

Nick Enright
BLACKROCK
At a surf club party, a 15-year-old girl is raped and murdered. As the community tries to deal with the aftermath, a boy struggles with the difficult choice between loyalty and truth.
0 86819 531 6

Trevor Graham
MABO: LIFE OF AN ISLAND MAN
Eddie Koiki Mabo's courtcase overturned the 200-year legal fiction that Australia was uninhabited prior to European arrival. He won for Aborigines and Torres Strait Islanders the right to claim

remaining Crown land in Australia, providing they could prove an unbroken chain of traditional ownership.
0 868 19 580 4

P.J. Hogan
MURIEL'S WEDDING

Muriel, an unhappy young woman in dismal surroundings, starts her quest to overcome obstacles like her family, her joblessness and her obsession with the music of ABBA—and leap into the unknown. The best revenge is success!
0 868 19 429 8

Baz Luhrmann/Craig Pearce
STRICTLY BALLROOM

The exuberant story of a struggle for love and creativity in a world limited by greed and regulation.The screenplay of the film that took the world by storm and won accolades for dancer Paul Mercurio and director Baz Luhrmann.
0 868 19 359 3

Melina Marchetta
LOOKING FOR ALIBRANDI

Adapted by the author from her award-winning novel. In the year Josie finishes high school, she discovers her family's past, meets her father for the first time and grapples with love, grief, identity and belonging. A sensitive story about an Italian-Australian girl at the brink of adulthood.
0 868 19 623 1

Hyllus Maris/Sonia Borg
WOMEN OF THE SUN

Four TV dramas about experiences of Aborigines since the coming of the first white people to Australia 200 years ago. The chief protagonist in each drama is a woman whose resilience in the face of despair and destruction gives fresh insight into the history of race relations in Australia.
0 868 19 081 0

Louis Nowra
COSÌ
Lewis, a first-time director, is hired by a psychiatric institution to direct a show as part of a therapeutic program. As Vietnam War protesters rage outside, Lewis and the cast find companionship and empowerment in ideals, as the real world appears rife with confusion.
0 86819 475 1

RADIANCE
Three half-sisters who have drifted far apart meet again at the ramshackle house on stilts where they grew up. They have come to bury their mother. This volume includes the original play, the screenplay and an essay from the author discussing the adaptation process.
0 86819 624 X

Nick Parsons
DEAD HEART
Adapted by the author from his award-winning play about the clash between white law and tribal lore on a remote Aboriginal reserve.
0 86819 459 X

Michael Rymer
ANGEL BABY
A tragi-comic love story set at the border of psychosis and sanity. When Harry meets Kate at a drop-in centre for the mentally ill, true love blooms. Guided by Astral the oracle, they strike out to create a home in the outside world.
0 86819 457 3

Stephen Sewell
THE BOYS
Adapted from Gordon Graham's controversial stage play, this is a powerful and affecting film script. A scarifying and unflinching analysis of the violence that lurks in the heart of Australian suburbia.
0 86819 569 3